Have Gavel Will Travel

A NATIONAL PARK JUDGE REFLECTS ON
TRUTH, JUSTICE, AND WHY EVERY JUROR
DESERVES A DOUGHNUT

ROBERT BRAITHWAITE

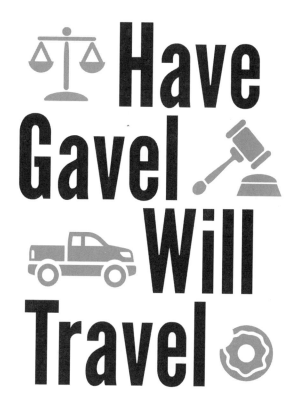

Have Gavel Will Travel

A NATIONAL PARK JUDGE REFLECTS ON
TRUTH, JUSTICE, AND WHY EVERY JUROR
DESERVES A DOUGHNUT

ROBERT BRAITHWAITE

PLAIN SIGHT PUBLISHING

AN IMPRINT OF CEDAR FORT, INC.
SPRINGVILLE, UTAH

ISBN 13: 978-1-4621-1593-8

Published by Plain Sight Publishing, an imprint of Cedar Fort, Inc.
2373 W. 700 S., Springville, UT 84663
Distributed by Cedar Fort, Inc., www.cedarfort.com

LIBRARY OF CONGRESS CATALOGING-IN-PUBLICATION DATA

Braithwaite, Robert, 1950- author.
Have gavel, will travel / Robert Braithwaite.
    pages cm
ISBN 978-1-4621-1593-8 (alk. paper)
1. Braithwaite, Robert, 1950- 2. Judges--Utah--Biography. I. Title.

KF373.B655A3 2015
347.73'2234--dc23
[B]

2014038073

Cover design by Shaun McMurdie
Cover design © 2015 by Lyle Mortimer
Edited and typeset by Eileen Leavitt

Printed in the United States of America

10 9 8 7 6 5 4 3 2 1

To Alice Todd Braithwaite (1916–2014),
the best mother a child could ask for.

Contents

Acknowledgments

I would like to thank my wife, Arlene, and my children, Ally, Elaine, Nic, and Hope, for their support and encouragement.

I would also like to thank those who have read, edited, and commented on various drafts of this book: Dawn Marano, Rosalyn Eves, Mike Evans, Elaine Jolley, Andrea Hatch, Earl Mulderink, Stephen Trimble, Ted Stewart, Lynnae Allred, and Eileen Leavitt.

1 Canoodling Nudes and Dangerous Dudes

I **am relaxed and looking out at a wonderful Southwest** desert scene: coral sand, teal-gray sagebrush, and red sandstone cliffs, all under an ultramarine blue sky. Down below me, the deep, cold water of Lake Powell spreads flat and wide until it disappears into channels and slot canyons created by the distant cliffs. As far as "work on location" goes, this beats the courtroom hands down. My reverie is interrupted by my guide for the day.

"You can sit here in the summer and watch marriages dissolve."

I look over at Ranger St. Clair. We're parked on the Lone Rock Beach boat ramp, a corrugated swath of concrete a hundred feet wide that descends at a steep angle down into the lake. His national park SUV isn't exactly inconspicuous—official law enforcement markings on the sides, strobe light bar perched on top, radio antennae waving up high like the tail of a mutant bug in a sci-fi movie—the whole works. My son Nic would have loved this when he was five and a big fan of cops. Frankly, it *does* feel pretty cool to be sitting there in the front seat, on the lookout.

It's early May and still cold in the high desert, so no boats are on the ramp, and no one is camping on the beach. I'm a part-time federal magistrate judge in the national parks region of southern Utah. Since Lake Powell has just been added to my jurisdiction, the ranger is showing me the lay of the land before the waves of tourists swarm the beaches for the summer and jam the court calendar with criminal cases. Take three million visitors and not enough rangers, blend in alcoholic drinks, libidos,

1

and tempers, spread the whole lot unevenly over dozens of griddle-hot beaches, and the omelet tends to get burnt in spots.

The ranger points across the boat ramp. "The husband pulls a boat all the way from California without letting the wife drive. He gets in line to put his boat in the water, and then when it's his turn, he swings over there." He moves his hand from right to left in a sweeping arc, saying, "He brings the truck up to the top of the ramp, lines the truck and boat up straight so they're facing away from the water, jumps out, points to his surprised wife, and says, 'You back it up and I'll guide you.' Then all hell breaks loose."

"Because pulling a boat on a trailer is a piece of cake when you're driving forward, but backing one up is tricky," I guess.

"Yup. The wife tries her best, but the pressure's on. It's over a hundred degrees, people are waiting on her, air conditioners are going full blast, and engines are overheating. To top it all off, the husband is yelling, 'No, too far—cut it the other way,' and she overcorrects and he yells at her to straighten it out and try again. Maybe they even back it up enough so the husband is standing in the water, getting all wet and furious while the boat is at an awkward angle. It doesn't matter. At some point, the wife has had enough, gets out of the truck, throws the keys at him, and yells, '*You* do it!' and storms off to sulk and curse the day she ever married him."

"And so starts the family bonding."

"Happens all the time," the ranger says ruefully.

We have a lot in common, the ranger and I. We are both students of human nature, you might say, sharing this beat. What rangers see on a boat ramp, judges hear about later in court.

I hear only criminal cases, and many of those crimes occur in the national parks (Zion, Bryce, Capitol Reef, Arches, and Canyonlands) and monuments, as well as in the Forest Service and Bureau of Land Management lands, and national recreation areas like Lake Powell. The cases in the parks are mostly small change: marijuana possession, drunk driving, public nudity, and so on. But there are also a few bank robberies and a growing number of immigration cases on my docket every year. And since I-15 and I-70 are drug corridors, my area picks up a fair share of drug interdiction cases.

My court and the regional offices of the FBI, DEA, and ICE (Immigration and Customs Enforcement) are located in St. George near the southern border of the state. I live an hour north, in the place where I practiced law and raised a family. Before I got this job, I served a long stint as a state judge in a court of general jurisdiction, meaning I heard every kind of case ranging from parking tickets to capital homicides.

Lake Powell is home to mostly misdemeanors, but they take place over an immense area. So on the morning following my conversation with the ranger, I am up in the air in a four-passenger airplane with a bush pilot from Alaska. The head ranger at Powell has insisted the guy is a legend, the best bush pilot in the whole flippin' world, and that I *must* take the flight to understand what the rangers have to deal with geographically. Tourists pay good money to do this very thing. I have claustrophobia, so two hours earlier, I'd taken half a Xanax. The medication makes me feel lethargic and pleasant before entering the airplane. Without it I'd soon be swearing there wasn't enough oxygen to go around, which wouldn't impress my cohorts.

What I see in the two hours is wonderful: breathtaking scenery that is both beautiful and barren, both natural and otherworldly. Glen Canyon Dam backs up 185 miles of the Colorado River, creating Lake Powell. With a hundred or so side canyons accessible by boat, some of which are as long as twenty miles, the lake has nineteen hundred miles of shorelines for the rangers to patrol.

Everywhere we fly, we see the unnatural juxtaposition of standing blue water and desert. Laid out before us is a spectrum of orange, vermillion, red, coral, and white sandstone formations and cliffs sloping and dropping down into those side canyons. At the shoreline, the heat of the sandstone disappears under the cold Colorado River water. The water looks especially blue when abutting the orange sandstone, because, as my artist wife would explain, they are complementary colors that intensify one another by virtue of their proximity.

The scenes that glide by would be at least vaguely familiar to anyone who goes to the movies. Lake Powell is a favorite location for Hollywood directors. It's where Charlton Heston landed in *Planet of the Apes* (1968) and where he climbed Mount Sinai in *The Greatest Story Ever Told* (1965), and it's where *Hulk* (2003), and *Charlie's Angels: Full Throttle* (2003) faced down their diabolical nemeses.

Brent McGinn, the chief ranger at Lake Powell, or part of the Glen Canyon Recreation Area, as it is formally called, narrates as we go. "Judge, this is not like Zion or Bryce. We have forty full-time law enforcement officers here in the summer, and we need them. Zion has ten. Bryce has three. There you're mostly dealing with busloads of polite tourists from

Japan and Europe. Here, we're dealing with a lot of people who've come to get away from it all and cut loose. And they don't always commit the crimes near Page [the small city closest to the lake] or places where it's easy to take care of them

An armada invades Lake Powell every summer with watercraft ranging from inner tubes to speed boats to ninety-ton yachts with enough deck surface to house two helicopter landing pads.

"See that?" Brent says, pointing down to the main channel. "That's a tug boat pulling a container trailer." (Sure enough, there's a commercial maritime getup that looks like it belongs out on an ocean.) "It's headed for Dangling Rope."

"Dangling Rope?"

"Yup. There's a marina with a convenience store there. It's in the middle of the lake, only accessible by boat, and more ice cream, beer, and soda pop are sold there than any other convenience store in the country."

We arrive at Dangling Rope and circle above it as we look down at the store: a floating dock with empty berths awaiting summer arrivals; a few trailer houses for employees; and a fuel barge to supply gas to the boaters, since the marina is midway between the Wahweap and Bullfrog marinas. The store is a white metal box with small windows, a barnacle attached to the dock.

Further north, over open water, the pilot says, "See that brown boat down there?"

From a distance it looks like a wooden slave galley from *Ben Hur* (1959).

"It's a school boat. On the east side of the lake is Hall's Crossing Marina, and on the west side is Bullfrog Marina. The school boat takes the kids from Halls Crossing over to school in Bullfrog in the morning and brings them back in the afternoon. They've got twenty or thirty kids on each side, K–12."

We land on the bladed dirt runway near Bullfrog Marina, and Brent shows me the holding cells and small office for the rangers there. It's an austere, bare-bones operation: a phone, a computer, and a metal desk. But the equipment works (usually), and the rangers make arrests day and night, write reports, scan them onto the computer, and attach them to emails they send to my clerk and me. It's just as I always tell people, "I work seven days a week in the summer, but not for a full eight hours."

On the return flight, the pilot tells me there is an average of twelve deaths at Lake Powell each year, and he points out places where he's had to land on rescue attempts or to haul out bodies too far from the water to be conveniently transported by boat. "Some are heart attacks, some dehydration while hiking, and, of course, drowning. A lot of deaths are from dumb things people do after drinking too much or using drugs. Like driving a Jet Ski in the moonlight and hitting a sand bar at fifty miles per hour."

A short while later, he dips the right wing, and we veer offline to be closer to a shoreline. "That empty beach down there is called Bikini Beach. In the summer it's packed with sunbathers, and sometimes girls lift their tops and flash me."

I twist around in my seat to address Brent behind me. "And you had me come in *May?*"

"That's right," he says, grinning. "We can't have a judge seeing *that.*"

Southern Utah is attractive to retirees and to happily married couples (unlike the couple at the boat launch) who are finally getting around to building their dream homes. Some come for the mild winters in St. George, some to be near the scenery, and many come just to get to a smaller town after living in much larger cities. But dreams, as I've learned being a judge here, aren't always a sure bet. Often they're subject to the shortcomings of the dreamers or the permanent challenges in life.

Suppose you find yourself in a lawsuit situation similar to one of my former plaintiffs. You come north from Las Vegas to scout out a site for your second home, and you find a location with spectacular views into Zion National Park. From your front porch you can see soaring red sandstone cliffs topped with evergreen Ponderosa forests. You build a log cabin. Not an "Abe Lincoln" log cabin, mind you, but a beautiful trophy home with unique (read: expensive) features and accessories to suit your until-now deferred desires.

But there is a problem: a dispute arises between you and the builder as to the soundness of the structure itself. You end up in the state court where I used to work for a hard-fought two-week jury trial. The jury decides the case; my role is just to see that the trial proceeds fairly, kind of like an umpire at a baseball game. You win a substantial judgment. But then the defendant, the builder, files bankruptcy, and there are appeals and, well, we all know court cases aren't wrapped up neatly in one hour like on TV, don't we?

But the take-away for me personally from the case was the testimony offered by an impartial, matter-of-fact appraiser.

After the necessary nuts-and-bolts information by the witness about his extensive experience as an appraiser and the probable value of the intact home, the plaintiff's attorney delivered the *coup de grâce*.

"But this wasn't just any home, this was a *dream* home. What extra value does a dream home have?"

"None," the appraiser said matter-of-factly.

Determined, the plaintiff's attorney pressed on. "These people [motioning to the attractive couple at the plaintiff's counsel table] planned this home from the time they were poor newlyweds. Over the years, they researched and planned all its facets. They poured their dreams into it. Surely that adds significant value!"

"Not really," said the appraiser. "The home's value is what a willing buyer would pay a willing seller. Dream homes are just like any other house, really."

"I come across dream houses all the time in my work," the appraiser continued. "Sometimes the owners sell them because they have to move; sometimes they get bored with them and want to build another one, and of course, a lot of times they end up divorcing and have to divide the assets."

The mood in the room deflated. And I don't mean just the plaintiff's. I glanced around at the audience and then at the jury during the brief silence. There were a lot of disappointed expressions and furrowed brows. Even *I* found this news depressing.

But then, I've learned that dreams—*including dream vacations to national parks*—are subject to the shortcomings of the dreamer. If you're a chauvinistic jackass who gives your wife a difficult job in front of an impatient audience, then you're likely to stay a jackass. The fact that you're standing knee-deep in Lake Powell isn't going to baptize you into a decent spouse.

Lest I be accused of sermonizing, my family would be happy to testify that I'm completely capable of bad dream vacation behavior myself. Once upon a time, after a long day in a cramped rental car, my wife and I and our four kids stopped for a late meal in a roadside diner. The food was unexpectedly wonderful. Tummies were filled and thirsts quenched. Spirits lifted. Goodwill abounded. Main courses cleared, we ordered a round of deserts. Who needs a budget? Separate five-dollar pieces of cake or pie for everyone!

I chose my favorite, banana cream pie, which arrived looking as if it had been taken warm from my mother's oven, with real whipped cream and sliced bananas. That's when I noticed my family eying my dessert instead of their own and remembered the french fries they'd all filched from my hamburger combo-meal at lunch—these same people who'd claimed *they* didn't *want* french fries. The heck they didn't!

"No one gets to eat this but me!" I heard myself announce. Then I proceeded to spit on my pie. Not a throat chunk, mind you, just a delicate mist.

I looked around at my family in satisfaction, only to encounter identical expressions of disgust on the faces of my wife and kids. I looked down at my pie. I didn't want it any more. Some jerk had spat on it.

How does a pie-spitter end up as a judge in his own backyard? Well, not because of a master plan, if I'm any example. I drew a lousy military draft number of forty-nine in 1969, stayed in college, and majored in political science because it was the sixties and I found the subject fascinating. As I approached graduation I thought, "What the hell do I do with *this* degree?" The answer, of course, was nothing—many in my graduating class had the same degree and there were no jobs.

So I went to law school. There I encountered the Socratic method, which made me wonder if, perhaps, trying to repel the Tet Offensive wouldn't have been preferable. Under the Socratic method, Professor Snarky asks Jimmy and Susie what they think the *holding* in a case means. When Jimmy and Susie answer, Professor Snarky challenges their answers, so as to force them to think rationally. Or so goes the theory. What actually happens is that Jimmy gives answers and the professor says, "No, that's not right," and Susie gives it a try and the professor says, "That's not even close," and after an hour the other students leave the classroom wondering what the right answers were. As *Black's Law Dictionary* notes, "Socrates himself did not profess to be capable of teaching anything, except consciousness of ignorance."[1] Message received: the teacher is brilliant, and we're a bunch of simpletons.

After that, I left law school, and—with no answers—I was unleashed on the public. I first hung up a shingle in my hometown. Then, after a while, the city attorney job came up, and I applied for that and was appointed, not because of my intelligence or integrity, but because I was the attorney that submitted the lowest bid. And, for the next ten years, each June when the city council opened tire bids to equip the police cars, I remembered, "Hey, that's how they chose *me*!"

People said I had a knack for being city attorney, and I could have enjoyed it forever, except an opening occurred in the court I frequented, and I thought, "Why not me?" I applied, and the governor said, "No, because you're too damn young!" (I was thirty-four; what was *his* problem?) But I was dogged and applied again when the position opened up a few years later and was appointed *without being the low bidder—hooray!*

I settled into the job of circuit and then district judge quickly, learning on the job just like I had as an attorney. My first jail sentencing occurred my first day on the bench. It was a drunken driving case, and I knew that two days jail was the standard in the district for a first-time offender. And I knew the reason—drunk drivers kill an average of more than 10,000 people a year in America.[2] However, believing a sentence should be of a certain type and actually imposing one are two different things. It felt alien to say, "You will serve this weekend in jail." Knowing that person will be deprived of their liberty is not a normal experience, and was a little unnerving at first. On the other hand, if waves make you seasick, you better stay on shore.

The second case provided a learning experience. It involved a charge of simple public intoxication. The man pled guilty.

"Is this your first offense?" I asked.

"Yes," he answered.

Before I could impose the fifty-dollar fine, my clerk cleared her throat, leaned toward me, and, in a stage whisper, said, "It's his seventeenth case just in this court."

Oh, I thought, as it all came into focus. *This is how it works. I ask questions, and they lie to me!*

I never actually sat down and thought about my judicial philosophy before applying to be a judge. I mean, teachers teach, and judges judge, right? I had spent enough time in courtrooms to know how I wanted to run things, and my goal was to be fair to the people who came before me. But I couldn't have put what I believed into words until I attended a judicial seminar a couple of years after my appointment.

A full day had been set aside for representatives of each level of Utah state courts to meet with a nationally renowned expert on judicial administration and philosophy. We convened in Salt Lake City. We were supposedly the bright lights (fancy that!) from our levels of court, and our task was sorting out the goals of the judiciary in the state of Utah.

There were about thirty of us in the room, and we met in plenary sessions and breakout groups: thinking outside the box, discussing paradigm shifts and seven basic principles of jurisprudence. Everyone seemed to have higher IQs and broader vocabularies than I did, and after a while my head started hurting. I stopped talking and instead thought about a mountain meadow while intellectual eagle-thoughts voiced by others soared over my earth-tethered head.

Near the end of the day, after lots of discussion, we had arrived at only one partial tenet—the goal being to have seven, if I recall correctly. Before adjourning, the facilitator asked if there were any more comments and then looked at me. "You haven't said anything Judge Braithwaite. Care to at least share *some* thoughts?"

Irritated at his tone, I said, "Yeah. How about we forget about all of this, and just adopt as our goal, 'convict the guilty, free the innocent, and place the kids in the right home?'"

"I guess that's *one* thought," he said dismissively and moved on.

As we dispersed after adjournment, a judge came up to me and said, "I understood what you were saying, and I agree with you." He was a judge I admired, so his comment meant a lot to me. There'd been some chuckling after the presenter and I sparred, and I wasn't sure if the other judges had sided with him or with me. There were probably judges in both camps.

Over the years, I thought about that encounter and wondered if maybe I inadvertently wrote the epitaph for my own headstone that day. While the goal I stated had been a spur-of-the-moment reaction, I think the confrontation unearthed what I believed at my core, and I said what I did without any forethought or polishing. By the end of my state career, I could honestly claim that I *strived* to convict the guilty, free the innocent, and place the kids in the right home.

Over a sixteen-year career as a state judge, I heard whatever came up, ranging from parking tickets to divorce to rape to murder. It was an important position, and the cases were interesting, but over time I felt like I was becoming impatient and worn down by the continual stream of problems and crimes. I had had enough, and I retired a few years after I became eligible.

No more civil cases with attorneys quibbling over whether interrogatory #163 was answered honestly or not. No more horrific rape cases, no new photos of bloated corpses with dark stab wounds, or bloodied butcher knives used to stab a murder victim to be seared into my brain. No more divorce cases that had me tossing and turning in bed, worrying if I'd put the kids in the right home. And mostly, no more deciding if a murderer lived or died.

When I qualified for retirement, I finished out the final six-year term the voters had elected me to and called it a day. I might note that in Utah the governor appoints and the voters determine if the judge stays or goes. It's not perfect, but I think it is the best system to minimize politics entering into judicial elections. Voters vote based on records, not promises, and there is no fund-raising or campaigning.

As I neared retirement, I knew that the part-time US magistrate judge position was coming open in St. George and I applied. I was lucky enough to get the position shortly after my retirement. I enjoy the work, and it keeps me busy.

These days, I hear only criminal cases: misdemeanor trials and the front-end of felonies. It might sound as though I've opted for a backwater—I have—but it's never boring, and sometimes I even hear cases involving the president of the United States. Seriously. (More on that later.) Let my bosses, the lifetime-appointed district judges, handle the felony trials and the sentencings and the myriad civil trials until they, too, decide they need a good night's rest.

Once a month I travel 250 miles north to Salt Lake City to hear the Fur, Fang, Feather (F3) calendar that has accumulated and visit with the other judges, all of whom sit in Salt Lake City. The calendar was named by Ron Boyce, a legendary law professor-turned-magistrate judge, who coined the moniker after noting the preponderance of the cases brought in by the forest service and the fish and game and wildlife officers. The victims of most F3 crimes haven't been traumatized, and every time I enter the expansive old courtroom on Main Street I'm grateful for that.

From where I sit on the bench in Salt Lake City, I'm always a little awestruck over the standing-room-only assemblage. The assembly is mostly people charged with misdemeanors, but it also includes the cops that cited them, witnesses, and attorneys. Every chair—even those in the jury box—is taken, since no jury of peers is required in F3. As judge, I'm the final arbiter. The faces staring at me are fearful and angry—the misdemeanants are nervous and unhappy since they don't want to be there, and sometimes look ready to rebel. I feel like Dr. Frankenstein's monster before the village welcoming committee. One of us is not the same as the others—and the others are on edge because they don't know what I might do to them. Thankfully, because of the security screening in the foyer, there's nary a torch or pitchfork in sight.

Once I've entered, there's nothing to be done but to plunge ahead. "Listen up!" I say. "We've got eighty cases in the next three hours, and I'm not giving this speech eighty times. Each of you here has the right to not make any statement against your own self-interest. Any statement you make can be used against you . . ." and on and on I go, telling them the rights they already know from watching cop shows on TV.

I have a system for running my F3 calendars: shackled defendants in jumpsuits go first. No felons on this calendar mind you, just a few misdemeanants who've violated probation and have been hauled in on an arrest warrant. Security is always on my mind—it's tight, but I don't want to be the judge in charge when things go south. For example, when a desperado does something desperate, like try to escape.

I also call incarcerated cases first so the transportation officers can go about their business shuttling the different inmates from holding cells to the various courtrooms. Once the incarcerated defendants have been dealt with, I hear the large balance of the cases remaining. Most of these cases can be dispatched quickly, leaving the lengthiest hearings for after lunch. This organizational strategy of mine allows the largest number of people to get back to their lives in the shortest amount of time.

Contrary to what you might expect, the attorneys appreciate this practice. They want to get back to their offices and get to work on cases waiting for them there. When I first started as an attorney back in the '70s, I appeared before a judge who, in my opinion, didn't manage his calendar efficiently. Rumor was that he liked to ensure a large audience for as long as possible. Opinions varied on this. But as a result, many an attorney had to spend all day waiting for a ten-minute hearing. Everyone was instructed to show up at one appointed time—hence the standing room only situation—and if you were not there when your case was called, you were called "out of order," and your case was stricken for the day—not the result you or your client was after.

One by one, according to the court calendar, I invite the public forward; I describe their particular charges and the penalties that might ensue. A man wearing new slacks, a pressed dress shirt, and a sport coat comes forward. He could be anything: doctor, lawyer, shoe salesman. Whatever his occupation, he's accused of killing a deer when he wasn't supposed to. He preempts anything I might say by forcefully announcing, "I want a trial!"

"Not a problem," I say. "That's what we're here for. Do you want your trial the afternoon of August twelfth or September fifteenth?"

"You mean I have to miss work? I'm already missing work."

"Your call."

"But if I just explain it to you, you'll see the case should be dismissed!"

"I can't do that anymore than I could just listen to the officer and convict you without a trial. I have to hear from both sides at a trial."

"This is ridiculous. I'll just pay a fine and be done with it!"

I'm relieved. He's blustery and posturing while he talks and stares around the courtroom, sizing up people who catch his attention. In short, he's the kind of guy who would chafe at following any kind of procedural decorum in a trial, and I'd have to be constantly bringing him back into line to maintain order. I've had enough of those trials—thank you very much—so I say, "Okay the fine is . . ." and then move on to the next case, which deals with cutting, removing, and damaging trees without a permit. A guy wearing dirty Levi's, a checkered flannel shirt, and boots—in short, he's dressed like he's auditioning for the role of Paul Bunyan—saunters up to the podium with an expression that clearly says, "This is bullshit. I can cut down trees if I want." He pleads not guilty, and we give him a trial date. Then a series of marijuana possession cases come up. This could be anybody. Today it's mostly college-age kids, but I've seen all ages and professions from graying hippies with portable oxygen tanks to a group of energetic and athletic public defenders from Minnesota who liked to hike and then sit around the campfire and relax with a joint.

Some defendants plead not guilty, and we set a date for trial; some plead guilty and are sentenced on the spot. I honestly don't know which is worse: walking out with a sentence or rolling the dice and having a trial. I've never been on trial. Not that I haven't been charged. I once took my son Nic to Scottsdale, Arizona, to watch some San Francisco Giants spring-training games. We set off for the stadium one afternoon with ample time to get there, but I got lost. I refused to stop and ask directions, *knowing* I was on the right path when I passed a familiar 7-Eleven gas station yet again. I clenched the steering wheel and quickly cut a mid-block U-turn, noticing too late that I was executing the maneuver right in front of a cop.

He stopped me and asked if I knew why he had pulled me over. I decided to salvage something out of the situation by being a good role model for my son. I was polite to the cop, confessed everything, apologized, promised to pay the ticket on time, and threw in some extra "sirs" for good measure.

As we drove away my son said, "Boy, *that* was embarrassing!"

"Oh, no, Nic," I preached. "Anybody can get a ticket. It happens."

"Not that," he said. "It was embarrassing what a wuss you were with that cop!"

Shocked by his comment, I had to reasses my conversation with the cop. I concluded that, while not arguing was a good example to set for my son, turning into one of those puppies that flop on their back while wagging their tail to show they aren't a threat hadn't been an admirable parental move on my part. Sometimes being judged by teenage children is more brutal and challenging than being judged by a jury of your peers.

At 10:30 a.m., halfway through the F3 calendar, I call the next defendant. A nondescript man in his mid-thirties rises in the gallery and begins to walk forward.

"Actually, judge, there is a companion case," the prosecutor interjects. "Can you call . . ." and he says a woman's name, so I call her case as well. An equally nondescript woman in her thirties joins the man at the podium. They share a warm smile, and I read the charges aloud.

"Each of you is charged with public nudity in a national forest," I say.

Ka-pow! The audience snaps out of their boring-seminar-coma and a few titters reach the ears of the defendants. They stand a little straighter and glance backward over their shoulders in what I take to be pride. Until now they've been unremarkable participants in a courtroom parade, but now the audience is giving them a second look, and they're practically preening. Heck—*I'm* giving them a second look. But it doesn't last long. What I see are a man and woman who are neither beautiful nor ugly, tall nor short, fat nor skinny. I have no desire to see or imagine either of them naked, but I'm happy that they don't feel that way about each other. They just shouldn't go *au naturel* near a public campground. They're pleased as punch to pay a modest fine and go on their way.

As I forge through an F3 calendar, I try to focus on the individual standing before me at the walnut-veneer podium. I figure if it was me standing there, I would want the judge to treat me politely and answer my questions, not waste my time with speeches and folderol. My goal is to maintain a polite atmosphere and run things efficiently: here's what you're changed with, here's what the penalty would be if you plead guilty, and here's how long you'll have to pay a fine. Or plead not guilty, that's fine. There are no questions asked, and here's a trial date. If they plead guilty, they walk out with an address telling them where to send the money and a review date to make sure the fine is paid.

I address everyone—attorneys and defendants—as Mr. Jones or Ms. Jones. No first names. It's not fair to call *some* people by their first names and not others. This keeps the proceedings moving, and people are generally appreciative and polite. Those times they aren't, I adjust accordingly. Usually a stern look or a change in my voice is enough to get people to dial it back. Contempt power—punishment on the spot, basically—is exercised to control the court only in extreme situations, as I'll explain in a later chapter.

Minutes pass. Hours pass. We eat lunch and hold the short afternoon trials. Every now and then I glance up at the whole courtroom. It's like watching one of those vintage moving picture books, your thumb flipping pages, delivering a series of snapshots or cartoons: first the whole place is jammed, and then the hallway is emptied as defendants and relatives fill vacated seats in the courtroom proper. The courtroom is three-quarters filled, then half filled. Finally, it's just me, my clerk, and the attorneys handling the last case. I smile and say, "Well, that does it. See you next month." And they say, "Thanks, Judge. Drive carefully," and I head for the door.

I turn right down one hallway, then left down another, then proceed into an empty warren of law clerk's offices, and finally emerge into a spacious, abandoned judge's chambers. Congress has taken years finding a replacement for the last departing judge, so these are my squatter's quarters: floor-to-ceiling empty bookshelves, a desk with chair, and two chairs across from it for the infrequent visitor. No one has vacuumed or dusted the place in some time.

Home is still hours away, and I'm on the move. I snatch up my briefcase, checking to make sure the magnetic security passes are easily accessible in the outside pocket so I can quickly clear the building and parking lot and get on the freeway onramp. I'm often just early enough to position myself on the crest of rush-hour traffic, riding the traffic surf south as the commuter waves progressively dissipate into the Wasatch Mountain foothills.

Once I turn the corner at Santaquin, it's rural freeway for almost two hundred miles: cruise control on seventy-five and satellite radio—NPR, CNN, ESPN, Giants games, Jazz games—all the way home.

Midway I stop at Cluff's Carhop Café in Fillmore for a grilled cheese sandwich, fries, and a large Fresh Lime (7UP, ice, lime wedges, and—available at your finer western drive-ins—a maraschino cherry with a little cherry juice dripped in). The place blends into the decaying backdrop of old Highway 91 if you don't know it's there—fading red and gray checkerboard cinderblock, small, unobtrusive sign, gravel parking lot, all set back and ready to be missed at forty miles per hour. But it's welcoming and funky inside with old Utah license plates carpeting one wall and a shelf loaded with antique soda bottles on the other (Nesbitt's, 7UP 1976 Bicentennial, Bubble Up . . .). Much as I like the décor and food, I'm there for the fries: fresh potatoes, cut full length with a mini-tub of fry sauce (a Utah staple consisting of ketchup and mayonnaise) for dipping.

In my RAV-4's soft-drink holder there is usually a waxed cup of Dr. Pepper with no lid or straw but lots of ice, so that as evening darkens the horizon, I can chew the ice to stay awake. On the rare occasion *that* doesn't work, I suck an ice cube clean, pop it into my hand, and drop it down the back of my shirt. Pow—that will wake you up!

My boss (also a friend) thinks I do a good job, but often introduces me by saying, "It's not a coincidence that Judge Robert Braithwaite and Judge Roy Bean (the Old West judge known as 'the law west of the Pecos') share the same initials." It's not an entirely fair comparison. I mean, I share Bean's lack of fondness for lengthy hearings and legal hair-splitting, but I've never pocketed fines or held court in a saloon. Still, the comment is made in jest, so I respond in kind. "You city judges are too slow and anal-retentive," I retort. "A dose of frontier justice once a month is just what Salt Lake needs."

Frontier justice is just what I like doing. I dispense it in four locations: Salt Lake City, my home base in St. George—a modern facility that I will describe in the next chapter—Moab, and Big Water. In Moab, the reputed mountain biking capital of the world, I use a courtroom in a state court-house to hear cases mainly arising in Canyonlands and Arches National Parks. Big Water (population 417) is located on the border between Utah and Arizona, and we hear Lake Powell cases. Court is held in the town hall (a colleague describes it as basically a Quonset hut) located at 115 Aaron Burr Drive. If there's another street named for Burr, the former vice president who killed Alexander Hamilton in a duel and then fled to the West, I'm not aware of it. The name of the town and the drive were picked by the colorful founder of the town: the late Alex Joseph. A former police officer and a polygamist (one wife was the town attorney), Joseph served as the town's first mayor. The town doesn't charge us a fee, and sometimes people show up for court just to watch for entertainment.

And I don't blame them. They're students of human nature just like Ranger St. Clair and I at our observation post back on the boat ramp. With all my time judging cases arising out of the national parks, I've observed that most of us come to these parks for similar reasons: to water-ski at Lake Powell, to take in the spectacular scenery, to fulfill a dream vacation (or fail trying), or to canoodle with our honey. This isn't to say that a trip to the national park is going to land you in the courtroom in front of me. I only see the exceptions—those whose dreams and actions take them too far, and they end up in court the same as if they were back home. Mostly people come to the nation's parks and forests to spend valuable time with family and friends while enjoying some of the most spectacular scenery on earth. I get to do all of that (well, at least most of it), plus it provides me with a job. Like my boss once said: "You have the best job in the judiciary: night court in the national parks.

NOTES

1. *Black's Law Dictionary*, 7th ed. (St. Paul: West Group, 1999).
2. Matthew Chambers, Mindy Liu, and Chip Moore, "Drunk Driving by the Numbers," United States of Department of Transportation, accessed October 15, 2014, http://www.rita.dot.gov/bts/sites/rita.dot.gov.bts/files/publications/by_the_numbers/drunk_driving/index.html

2   Trying Papa

The judge is sitting on the ground, disheveled and confused. A boy looms above him. "That's not a backhoe; it's a *Bobcat!*" the boy says for the third time that morning.

The exasperated child is Jack, the judge's four-year-old grandson. The judge is me. On Mondays, I sit on the judicial bench. On Tuesdays, I sit in the turtle sandbox, or on the ground because that's where Jack wants me. I watch two of my grandchildren once a week while my daughter works as a part-time chemistry professor at the local university. When I watch them, I'm not a judge—I'm Papa.

I'm wearing my male nanny (*manny?*) uniform: sneakers, a clean white T-shirt, and dirty blue jeans. Jack is wearing pretty much an identical outfit. The only difference is that Jack's jeans were clean when he arrived, and mine are dirty because they're old Levi's, and this is the only occasion I wear them. Why wash them when they're just going to get dirty again? Jack certainly doesn't care.

Jack is the hands-on *'struction worker* (as he puts it), and I am the minimum-wage laborer in a project of breathtaking ambition. What happens is this: Jack gathers the miniature construction equipment provided by his grandparents. (Some kids are into dinosaurs, and others are into Legos. This kid adores *John Deere,* the name stamped on all the equipment and even on his cap.) The project begins by the carport along a retaining wall and extends in a curve to a rock-and-dirt hillside. When Jack's really feeling adventurous, it expands into the vacant lot behind the house.

He uses exact terms memorized from his children's books about such equipment, and takes on a 'struction worker manner, jutting his lower jaw out a cog and forcing his voice as low as it will go. And he corrects me. If I say "steam shovel," Jack says, "No, that's a mass excavator," and if I say, "dump truck," Jack actually says, "No, it's an articulated dump truck" (meaning that it has a hinge between the cab and dump box rather than being on one frame).

I welcome my role as apprentice. I like being the person making the calls in court, deciding which legal terms will be used in jury instructions, which motions will be granted and which denied, and, frankly, I enjoy the respect I receive as a judge (I mean—who wouldn't like being called *Your Honor?*). But that can be a little ego-inflating as well as stressful, and so today I play a different role in a different place, with someone else in charge.

I mostly sit in the dirt handing and taking back the various pieces of equipment as directed, kind of like a nurse assisting a surgeon. Except instead of yelling "scalpel," this surgeon yells "mini-loader," and instead of being scrubbed up and masked, this one is belly-down in the dirt, body extended, his face five inches from the toy being manipulated. To say he is *prone* is an understatement. He has *fused* with the ground.

At one point Jack abruptly sits up, a bewildered look on his face. "What do you want to be when *you* grow up, Papa?"

This question, seemingly plucked out of the air, leaves me speechless. *Why is he asking me this?* I wonder. Then I realize Jack knows what his mother does because he's been to her office and watched her grade papers at night. He knows what his father and his other grandfather do because he's been to the family drugstore and has seen them filling prescriptions as pharmacists. He has never seen me do anything except tend, dressed like him, doing the same thing that he does. To Jack, I am not a part-time judge, I'm a huge, balding four-year-old with bad joints.

"I'm a judge," I say. Jack looks at me like I've just spoken in tongues. While I'm trying to think of how to explain to a four-year-old what that word means, Jack loses interest and starts to move to a new construction site.

"What do you want to be?" I call after him.

Without hesitation, Jack yells over his shoulder, "A 'Sweet Child O' Mine' singer." This is not exactly the kind of response you expect from a four-year-old. Not even one who can pronounce the phrase *articulated dump truck*. His response makes me laugh. Not backhoe operator? Not road engineer? Really? Axl Rose? Must be from listening in when his dad cranks up hard rock CDs on road trips. I learned something about Jack that day, but the exchange leaves me feeling like he doesn't really know me as well as I'd like. I feel misunderstood.

When Jack's mother, Elaine, picks him up, I relate the story to her and say I'd like to have Jack come to court one day so he'll have some idea of what I do.

"We'll have to do that," she says.

Time passes, and the desire for such a visit percolates below the surface, finally breaching when I move into my new courtroom. "How about bringing the kids to St. George and seeing the new courthouse?" I ask. We pick a date, and she arranges to visit right after lunch.

Elaine brings both Jack and his sister Halle, a deceptively cherubic-looking two-year-old. She's a bright ball of energy with a face so round it looks like it could have been drawn with a compass, framed by a froth of curls. Wanting to make a good impression on my grandkids, I show them my brand-new chambers and furniture. They're not impressed. Apparently, they've seen chairs and desks before. But Halle is moved—literally—when she sees the toilet in my bathroom.

"I need to go potty," she announces.

Then it's time to work, and I show them the way to their seats. I tell them to stay in the courtroom as long as they can, but if they need to be noisy to be sure to go out in the lobby.

A minute later, I enter from the big oak door in the back.

"All arise," the bailiff says. "Court will resume; the Honorable Robert T. Braithwaite presiding." I scan the audience, which today includes my progeny. I look at them warmly. Surely Jack must be impressed with me, what with everybody standing when I enter the room and hearing that I am honorable—the man with the gun said so! I cross my fingers that things will go smoothly because this is a brand-spanking new courtroom, and not all of the bugs have been worked out. They did a trial run a week earlier, and it went fine, but final technological bells and whistles were installed the night before, and there wasn't time to check out the changes.

Settling into my seat, I look down at my files, read the name of the first case, and lift my gaze to address the congregation. Then I freeze. There is a face less than twelve inches from my own, a slack-jawed, double-chinned, aging moron carrying more flesh on his face than the bone structure was intended to carry. The only thing that prevents me from throwing him out is his familiar saggy-lidded eyes.

Everyone in the courtroom is staring at me with my stage fright. I have their attention and not in a good way.

"I'm looking at a picture of me looking at me and talking to me as I talk to you," I say. In fact, *all* of the computer screens located throughout the courtroom are now live, and, like the one in front of me, they're filled with the image of my startled face. The cameras apparently are voice activated.

"That's okay, Your Honor," the prosecutor says as the screens flip to a picture of him. "When I speak, the camera behind me kicks in, and the screen in front of me shows a picture of the bald spot on the back of my head."

This ultra-modern courtroom was wired for computers just last week. The screens are everywhere: one each for the judge, the clerk, and one for every juror, attorney, and witness. From my perspective, it looks like an airplane, peeled open during an in-flight movie—a home movie no less. The worst kind.

I place one hand on each side of the monitor in front of me and shove it aside so I can't see myself. I proceed to take the guilty plea of a man charged with interstate transportation of stolen firearms—a felony charge with a potential sentence of five years in prison.

The legal train starts chugging down the track, and I begin to relax. Jack's mom, Elaine, is on the back row of the gallery bench seats. The kids are squirming but under her control. *We can do this.* I commence the colloquy—the prescribed, formal dialogue—with the next defendant.

"I have before me a document entitled, 'Statement in Advance of Guilty Plea,'" I intone. "It appears to have a signature on page seven—is that your signature?"

"Yes," the defendant says.

Beep!

"What's that?" I blurt out. I look at the clerk. She shrugs. Fifteen seconds later there's another beep.

"I feel like I'm piloting a submarine. Can you do something about the beeping?" I ask.

The clerk says, "The technicians were here last night putting in final touches, but I think I can fix it."

Attorneys are waiting to finish their hearings in this courtroom so they can head to another court. The always-in-demand Spanish interpreter checks her watch because she is wanted in another courtroom, and I know I need to use her while I can. Most of all, I know my grandkids are on a short fuse, so I forge ahead, sonar sound effects notwithstanding.

"Did you first read the entire document," I ask the defendant, "each and every paragraph?"

I glance from the defendant to the gallery. Halle is running wind sprints on the back bench seats! She is smiling, having a grand time. Elaine grabs her and Jack makes a break for the aisle, but she corrals him with an impressive extended-leg move and hooks him in toward her other arm. She's gone all octopus to subdue her children. *Focus!* I tell myself. *Focus!*

The attorneys and defendant are staring at me because I've stopped talking, my mouth agape.

"Excuse me," I say, regrouping. "Let me start over. Did you first read each and every paragraph above your signature line before signing this document?

"Yes."

"And don't take this personally,"—*Beep!*—"because I have to ask everyone this: are you under the influence of any alcohol or drugs, including prescribed medications from a doctor, that would affect your judgment at this time?"

Jack is now inspecting a lint ball in the corner of the gallery.

"No."

"Have you had adequate time to speak with your attorney about this agreement and about your case in general?"

"Yes."

My script automatically rolls off my tongue thanks to years on the bench. But my attention isn't fully on the courtroom. Part of my brain focuses on the colloquy underway, but part of my brain registers that my daughter—*Beep!*—has lost the battle. The kids won't sit still, instead checking out the railing and testing the bench cushions for bounce-ability from various heights, while verbalizing their discoveries to each other. And why shouldn't they? One's four years old and the other two, for heck's sake. I've set my daughter up for failure by encouraging her to bring the kids to court.

I raise my hand, palm forward like a traffic cop, and the attorneys stop speaking. (I've never used my gavel. It's not my style.) The defendant deserves a better judge than he's getting right now. *Beep!* So does the prosecution. We're dealing with an eventual sentence likely to be five years. *The case!* I think. *The case!* This courtroom doesn't need a grandpa; it deserves a judge.

"I'm sorry," I say, while looking directly at my daughter, "you'll need to take the children out." I smile to let her know I'm not mad. She leaves, I can concentrate, and we finish the calendar. As I exit the courtroom I tell my clerk, "Call Salt Lake. They've gotta send a tech down to kill that beep."

Back in chambers, concerned that my daughter might be feeling bad, I dial her cell phone number. No answer, so I leave a message: "I hope you're okay," I say. "This was my mistake, not yours. I love all of you." I ask her to call me. Then I text her the same message, just to be safe.

An hour later, when she is home, she calls, fighting back tears. Unbeknownst to me, she'd had a sleepless night and a horrible morning dealing with students' complaints. She'd put out that fire just in time to drive to St. George to come to court and be supportive of her father, only to have him humiliate her in front of the entire courtroom.

We each apologize profusely. She's still all choked up—convinced she's not the super-mom she's supposed to be.

I am surprised at her vulnerability. After all, she didn't crumble under the pressure when she did the oral defense of her doctoral dissertation while eight months pregnant. The first two sentences of which read, "Several families of magnetic materials have been synthesized and studied. These families stem from the successful $V[TCNE]_y \cdot zCH_2Cl_2$ (TCNE = tetracyanoethylene) room-temperature magnet." She's never been one to shrink in the face of an adversary, a fact borne out by her slightly bent nose—a remnant of her trademark physical play under the basket as her high school basketball team's center.

I shouldn't be surprised at her insecurity though, because I'm the same way. I do all I can to project confidence and make all the right decisions, but inside, I'm a bundle of insecurities, capable of errors just like everyone else.

Afterward, I wander down the hall to the chambers of Tom Higbee, a juvenile judge I've known since we were Jack's age. "Not that you're as dumb as me, but just a free word of advice: Don't have small grandchildren visit your court."

I tell Tom what happened. Tom knows not only me, but also Jack's other grandfather. He nods sympathetically as the story is told.

"So, bottom line," I say, "I wanted my grandson to have as complete an image of me as he does of his other grandfather, and he's ended up with this: Grandpa Evan gives people medicine to make them better, sits on the leadership stand at church, and dresses in a white smock. Papa sits in a room with bad people, banishes me from his presence, watches football on Sunday, and wears black."

Tom laughs. "I'm sure it's not that bad."

"You're right," I say. "It has an upside."

"What's that?"

"He knows I'm powerful. It's not just anyone who can make his mother cry."

I had wanted to show my grandson that I was grown-up, that I was important, that I was a *judge*, for Pete's sake. Oh, there'd been a moment when Jack had turned to his mother and said, "Hey, look—Papa's on all the computer screens!" Was that what I was after? I feel, well, judged by that clarity Jack brings to all things.

Is my goal to be important to my grandson, or to prove to my grandson how important I am?

How many people have ended up on the other side of the bench because (like the defendant today) they needed guns or money or drugs or physical dominance to prove, to themselves or those around them, how important they were?

Clearly the best way I can be important to Jack is to get back to where we were before. I don't know why it took a disastrous court day to realize that, simply, Jack is important to me, and I too want—and need—someone to play with. Sometimes just sitting in the dirt *is* enough. In fact, sometimes it's the best thing you can do. Buckling down in the dirt with Jack helps both my relationship with him, and my performance as a judge. In order to gain the perspective I need to tackle the docket with a fresh mind and renewed faith in humanity, I need to trade the robe for the T-shirt and jeans, help Jack with his road project above the retaining wall, and hand him the Bobcat when he needs it. Or is it called a skid steer?

3 Controlling the Courtroom

Someone will control your courtroom and it should be you. You're the judge."

I heard these words back in 1988 from an experienced trial judge during a two-week orientation for new judges at the National Judicial College. There were about thirty of us in the classroom. "I'm not talking about putting your thumb on the scales of justice; I'm talking about influencing the pace of proceedings, the level of respect shown participants, those sorts of things. If you think, 'Oh, that's not me; I'm more of a laid-back type,' then you will create a vacuum, and *someone* will fill the void." In a moment of clarity, I knew how much I needed his advice. My natural inclination is to be a counterpuncher, not the one who leads out at the opening bell.

One Friday afternoon as a state judge, I called the final case of a short misdemeanor calendar, feeling grateful I'd gotten through the week's cases and could start looking forward to the weekend. An elderly woman, wearing an old cardigan sweater over a simple housedress, approached the podium. Her husband sat in the back of the courtroom, his head bowed, the only person left in the audience.

I told her if she pled not guilty we'd have a trial, and if she pled guilty she'd have to pay a seventy-five dollar fine.

"I *want* to go to jail!" she demanded, pulling herself erect, looking me dead in the eye, her jaw set, hands gripping the podium.

Perplexed, I said, "But this isn't that serious of a crime. It's just 'Disturbing the Peace.' It says on the ticket you were yelling at your husband in your front yard so loud that the neighbors called the police."

"I want to plead guilty and go to jail."

"Well, I'm not going to do that," I said. "That sentence wouldn't fit the crime. You don't get to be the defendant *and* the judge." She left the courtroom, her husband tagging along. I gathered up my files and handed them to the clerk. Just as I was about to leave the bench, we heard a commotion in the lobby. In a few seconds the bailiff walked into the courtroom leading the woman by the elbow, then pivoted so the two of them faced me. "This lady just slugged the front window and cracked it."

I looked at her in disbelief. She couldn't have weighed more than 110 pounds, and it was a big plate-glass window.

"You did that?"

"Yes. You wouldn't put me in jail, and I can't stand being with that man one more minute!" she said, pointing back at her husband.

Domestic violence being a daily issue in my court, it was reasonable for me to ask if she was in fear of harm from him.

"No." She cradled her right fist in her cupped left hand, but seemed more angry than hurt since she was wiggling all her fingers.

"Well, in your frame of mind, I'm not going to turn you loose to do something else," I said. "So you win—I'm putting you in jail for the weekend."

"Good!"

"But you'll have to pay for the window."

"I wouldn't have to if you'd put me in jail like I told you in the first place!" she said with disgust.

I looked at the husband. Nothing there—a perfect poker face.

I never saw either of them in court again, and they were locals. There were no divorce proceedings, no domestic violence protective orders, not even a traffic ticket. It's just further proof that you can never guess what goes on behind closed doors in a marriage.

I had a remote and brooding father, a brilliant but tortured soul who cowed the family with his violent mood swings. He was often gone from home, thoroughly absorbed with his work. The vacuum created by his absence was fortunately filled in large part by two wonderful older brothers. I grew up vowing not to repeat my father's mistakes, and I knew at an early age that when I became a parent I wanted to control the atmosphere in my home as much as possible in a positive way and to avoid the toxic stress found so often in the home of my youth. I may or may not have succeeded. As my wise father-in-law once put it, "I vowed I wouldn't make the mistakes that my parents did, and I haven't. I've made *new* ones!"

Being a judge hasn't given me any advantage in running the household, as far as my wife and children are concerned. It was less than a week after I'd taken the bench that I was setting the record straight with my wife, Arlene, about something, and she interrupted me: "Don't use that Judge Voice here—just don't even try!" Damn, I wanted to. It felt so *good* at work!

To my children, I'm just Dad—a good guy who tries hard but sometimes overregulates things. My daughter Elaine and I were still arguing over curfews when she was a college freshman.

"Where have you been? It's past midnight."

"We were just having fun. Give me a break—it's not like I'm out doing drugs or something."

"I know. That's not what I'm worried about."

"We were playing hide-and-seek at Canyon Park."

"That's dangerous!"

"Riiight! Hide and seek is dangerous," she scoffed.

"It is if you're at Canyon Park at night! I arraign guys all the time for doing things at night in that park."

"There were ten of us. Nothing would have happened."

Elaine moved to her own apartment the next week. She was probably right, but what could I say? Presiding over thousands of criminal court cases *has* made me a little jumpy.

Elaine was six and Ally was eight the year I heard a jury trial in which a coed had been dragged under a tree and raped one night. It was not at a remote location, mind you, but right in the middle of the Southern Utah University campus, by the quad, just thirty feet from the theater building. The general area was well lit, there was a campus security phone a short distance away, and none of that made any difference when it happened. My daughters were taking ballet lessons in that same theater building at the time, so I did not miss the opportunity for a lecture the day I dropped them off in front of the building, dressed in pink tutus with their hair pulled back into little buns.

"I will be back. *Don't* leave this building during any breaks." I pointed to a tree and said, "Last month a girl was . . . ," and they rolled their eyes, and said in unison, "We know, Dad. You already told us!"

Not that being a parent who's also a judge is *all* bad. One day, when my daughter Ally was in high school, she came to me with a look of concern on her face. "Dad, we need to have a talk."

"Okay," I said. "What is it?"

"There's a problem with the boys I'm dating."

Concerned, I said, "What have they tried to do?"

"Nothing. It's *you*. They know you're a judge, so they're scared of you."

"That's not a problem," I smiled. "That's a good thing."

I don't think she agreed.

By the time our third daughter, Hope, came along, my wife, Arlene, and I were in our forties and more relaxed in our parenting—or maybe just more *weary*. But then, too, there was this sense that Hope had already beat the odds by surviving after her twin sister died six months into the pregnancy, and Arlene and I just enjoyed the privilege of being around her. Turns out exercising less control worked out just fine. (Or better than just fine.) As her sister Elaine has said, "Hope's one hundred percent spoiled and zero percent rotten."

Another day in court, a year or two after the rape incident, I had worked my way through a crammed criminal calendar from felony cases to misdemeanors. For safety's sake, the incarcerated felons were seated in the jury box, physically separated from family and victims watching in the audience, waiting for the transportation van to return. Dressed in orange jumpsuits with their hands and legs shackled, they made a strange-looking jury.

A parade of misdemeanants rose from the audience, walked to the podium, listened to their charges, and pled guilty or not guilty. Eventually, a soft-spoken young woman pled guilty to the relatively innocuous charge of underage drinking. I levied the standard $200 fine, and gave her two months to pay. No big deal, just one of the many cases that afternoon. It's a case I never would have remembered, except that as she started to leave, she thought better of it, returned to the podium, pointed a finger at me, and said, "F—— you!" Stunned, I said nothing for a second, then shrugged my shoulders, turned the palms of my hands upward, and said, "What?" There had been an audible gasp from the audience at her profanity.

"Not me—him!" she said, pointing at a shackled defendant sitting with the others in the jury box.

Confused, I took a closer look at the man she was pointing at—a savvy, courthouse frequent flyer in my assessment—who grinned at me like he'd just won the lottery without buying a ticket.

"Do you two know each other?"

"No," she said, and the defendant shook his head in agreement, but he was liking his new friend. She was nicely dressed in linen slacks, complimentary blouse, and was very attractive.

"You treated him with no respect," she said, swearing again. "It was disgusting."

The defendant had been charged with distribution of methamphetamine, and I'd simply advised him of his rights and set the case for a preliminary hearing the next week. I'd sentenced other defendants to prison that afternoon—I couldn't figure out why she was obsessing over *this* guy.

While she and I took turns speaking, the crowd in the courtroom had gone quiet, the way it does during match point, heads swinging back and forth in unison just like at Wimbledon.

I could sense a vacuum looming, and knew if I didn't do something soon I would lose control of the mood in the courtroom. I can't let people curse at me without consequence when they don't like my decisions, or I'd be in for an afternoon of f-bombs raining down. The felons in the jury box were especially attentive.

"I'm sorry, but you can't talk to me like that. I'm going to have you taken into custody," I said, motioning to the bailiff.

"I know," she said and walked proudly toward him.

"You think about how you want to act when you're here," I said. "I'll have you brought back tomorrow afternoon, and we'll review your situation."

The bailiff took her to the female holding cell, and I continued with the calendar long into the afternoon.

I didn't lose any sleep over my decision, but I was curious how she had behaved at the jail, so I had my clerk call the following day and tell the officer in charge to release her if there had been no further incidents. She hadn't acted out and was released.

I thought no more about the case until the clerk came into chambers the following week.

"Remember that girl you found in contempt? Her parents are in the lobby and want to talk to you."

"You know I can't do that," I said. I have a standing rule about not talking to people about cases. Judicial ethics forbids me from having discussions about a case with just one side present. Plus, there's no point. A mother isn't going to like the fact I put her kid in jail. A father isn't going to like the fact that I awarded custody to the mother. The examples are endless.

"I know," the clerk said, "but they seem nice, and they say they're sure you'll want to hear what they have to say."

I sighed. "Have them put it in writing. That way we'll have a record of what was said."

A half hour later I was reading the parents' note. In it they thanked me for locking up their daughter. They said she was a bright college student, but had serious mental health issues. She had refused to get any treatment for her disorder, and they feared for her life. Her stay in jail had made her realize she needed help, they said. Upon release she had finally relented to their requests and voluntarily signed into an inpatient mental health treatment center. They said it was all due to my handling of a challenging situation, and they thanked me.

Someone will control the courtroom, and the power to do so is given to the judge for a reason. For a fair and orderly process, it can't be delegated to an attorney with one side to represent, a litigant, and certainly not to an animated member of the audience. A judge does what he or she needs to do to maintain decorum and civility in the courtroom, and that expectation helps maintain decorum and civility in society at large. When we do what we must given the circumstances, exercise authority with an insistence on civility (and in the case of family life, with abiding love) things generally work out for the best.

4 Men in Black

No offense, but are you a real judge?" asked the tattooed defendant extradited from California. Normally, a comment like that would have received a sharp rebuke from me, but not this time.

Oh, there *had* been a time when I thought the trappings of the court were all a little over the top, a little too thespian, starting with the "all rise" for the guy dressed in a black muumuu at the front of the room looking down on the jurors, and the "Your Honor" this and that, and the "may I approach the bench" requests.

But a makeshift courtroom in a highway department building had since taught me that trappings *do* matter: that's why I just chuckled when the defendant took a look at the setup and asked his legitimate question.

My state court had been transferred out to the highway building back in the mid-90s so the regular courtroom could be gutted and rewired for the latest in computers and audio technology. The makeshift courtroom didn't have an elevated bench per se, just a four-inch-high platform for a desk and chair, jammed in a corner right by the door where I entered. Public seating consisted of folding chairs so that the room could be rearranged into a meeting room for the highway workers who generally worked in the building. The jerry-rigged arrangement didn't exactly communicate legal decorum.

Wearing the Uniform

Having people question my legitimacy shouldn't have surprised me, really. People need structure—rules to follow, lines marking in-bounds and out-of-bounds. They need referees in easily-recognizable uniforms to enforce the regulations. Not that a formal setting prevents bad behavior; it doesn't, but it does make it easier to recognize that rules need to be followed. The extradited defendant had obviously been in other courtrooms before, and it wasn't surprising that he had doubts about the authenticity of the one he had been brought to. As any good umpire knows, half the battle is being the guy wearing the uniform that says you are in charge. You call the shots. You interpret the rules.

Call It Both Ways—Innocent Until Proven Guilty

Being a judge has taught me that the person allegedly on the wrong side of the law deserves the presumption of innocence. Our entire criminal judicial system is based on proof beyond a reasonable doubt and the presumption of innocence. We need to know as much of the whole story as we can before we pass sentence. I've heard people make the startling claim, "He must be guilty or the police wouldn't have arrested him." Well, not so fast. One of the more bizarre examples that jumps to mind is the time I arraigned a swarthy tourist with a five-day beard. He'd been arrested on an outstanding felony warrant. I told him the charges and he said, "I didn't do it. I've never been here before. It must have been my twin brother."

The prosecutor chuckled and said, "Sounds far-fetched to me, but I'll check up on it."

The next day the prosecutor was back. "I did some research, and this defendant was telling the truth. He *does* have an 'evil twin,' so to speak. His twin has been arrested in other states and gives his brother's name and social security number. We move to dismiss the case."

A crucial difference between judges and umpires (and as a judge, I thank God for this difference) is that judges don't get heckled mercilessly. No one interrupts a trial to yell, "You need glasses," or "Call it both ways!" When tensions *do* run high, usually a judge can diffuse them with a sidebar conference, where the attorneys and the judge discuss matters at the bench quietly so the jury doesn't hear, or a visit with counsel in chambers. Or as a last resort, a judge can use contempt power to keep things from spiraling out of control. It's a power I'm glad I've only had to use a couple of times.

Many fans say that in the best-officiated games, you don't notice the referee or umpire, and the contestants themselves determine the winner without unnecessary meddling by the officials. But even good officiating doesn't always prevent heckling from people who don't know the rules.

Sometimes the Foul Gets Punished Without the Referee Blowing the Whistle

More often than we'd like, the supposed professionals—or at least people who should know better—prove to be capable of behaving very badly themselves. They get too passionate in their legal role and lose perspective. I'm thinking about the second day of a felony jury trial a few years ago. The defendant in the case had a long drug record and knew he was going to prison if he was convicted again. He'd chosen to hire a loud, aggressive lawyer to defend him against charges of distributing methamphetamine. You'll sometimes hear a person say—with pride—that they've hired "a real junkyard dog" for a lawyer. That's all well and good if the lawyer is also brilliant and well prepared, but too many times, laymen are impressed by an attorney who uses a booming voice and an intimidating manner to hide mental shortcomings or a lazy work ethic.

The attorney in this case, a large, florid man, liked to wear an American flag tie when appearing in front of juries. He also had a habit of filing pleadings that proved to be rewrites of earlier cases. While he'd change the headings of the documents, he'd often forget to change the guts of the documents, which made references to dates and places that had nothing to do with the case at hand. The guy was not only plagiarizing his own homework, but also being really sloppy about it.

The evidence against his client was strong, and so the attorney reached into his bag of tricks for a game changer. The final prosecution witness, a slender, soft-spoken bank teller, was on the stand, and the attorney was getting nowhere with his cross-examination. The longer she stuck to her story, the louder he boomed and the redder his face became. She was scared but unwavering. Exasperated, he dramatically backed up two steps, dropped to his knees, pressed his hands together under his chin like a praying supplicant, and said, "Now that I'm on my knees begging, will you tell the truth?"

I was furious because he was bullying the witness. I temporarily held my temper in check while I scanned the courtroom. The defendant chuckled and looked at his attorney with admiration. I looked at the jury. They were as repulsed as I was. No, I take that back. They were *more* disgusted than I was, and every face was glowering directly at the attorney.

He looked at them, and his smirk vanished. He scrambled to his feet, blustering, "No more questions."

Sometimes the foul gets punished without the referee needing to blow the whistle. As with sports and in theater, sometimes the supporting players also play a role in the mood or execution of an event in court.

The Rookie—"Fake It Until You Make It"

I was a little apprehensive the first time I put on my robe and took the bench. In addition to the normal rookie jitters, I'd made the mistake of confiding in friends that I was nervous, and they'd responded by claiming they were going to sit in the audience, rate my performance, and hold up flash cards like 1960s figure skating judges after each case. The clerk mercifully scheduled only four arraignments that afternoon, and when I entered the courtroom, I was relieved to see none of my so-called friends in the audience.

A case from that day stood out. A defendant pled guilty to drunk driving, and as I fumbled my way through the process, advising this and asking that, two parallel thought processes played out in my mind. My mouth was telling the defendant he could serve his mandatory two days jail on the upcoming weekend so he wouldn't miss work and to present himself to the Iron County Jail on Friday at 7:00 p.m. Simultaneously, my mind was wondering, *Is this really me? Now that I have this authority, do I really want to use it? Will this guy really show up, surrender his freedom, and be locked in a cell just because I say so? Is he going to see through this façade and realize that I'm just some rookie who still eats Cocoa Krispies and talks to himself when he drives?*

I'd steeled myself before entering court with the thought, *Act like you've been here before!* and used my best poker face so as to not give away my nervousness. A similar phrase I've heard since is, *Fake it until you can make it.* Luckily it only took a few days before I could stop *acting* like a judge and start being a judge. Since I acted like a judge, people treated me like one, and the role-playing process became ingrained. That's not to say I haven't stressed over decisions in hard cases—that's a different matter—but the worries of being accepted as a judge didn't last long.

That is, except for family of course. The first time an older brother, who'd led me to be a Giants fan, visited my court and the bailiff ordered everyone to rise, my brother remained seated and joked, "Even me? He's just my little brother!"

"Yeah, you too," the bailiff said.

Man, talk about feeling like a grown-up!

Back a few years ago—okay, a decade plus—I used to go to the university gym after work and on weekends to play pickup basketball games. Even at thirty-five (then forty, then forty-five) I was the old man on the court with the college kids. At the beginning of the school year, I'd get some candid feedback, such as, "Hey, blockhead, stop shooting so much." By the end of the school year, when I'd start a drive to the basket, I'd sometimes find a path open up, and I'd know the kid defending me had been in my court and wanted to make a good impression. It was then that I'd have to shut it down till next season. You have to *earn* the two points or it's no fun.

Eventually my knees gave out—a vertical leap left me high-fiving the bottom of the net instead of slapping the rim—and I gave up. But I've never forgotten one of the guys from those pickup games. He had played varsity for the basketball team and then stuck around a year or two after graduation. He came to the gym to just have fun, not trying to recapture lost glory like some ex-athletes. Accordingly, he played to the skill level of the other players in the game—at least until the end of the game, when he'd take over. This was good when he was on my team, and bad when he wasn't. I enjoyed playing with him; he didn't have the arrogance some ex-jocks do.

Then one day he showed up in my court, which shocked both of us. He didn't know I was a judge; I didn't expect to see him in shackles, charged with first-degree rape. I disclosed to both sides that I knew him a little and how. Both sides said that it wouldn't be a problem. This would be a jury trial; the verdict wouldn't be up to me.

The case arose when I was using the makeshift courtroom, so we held the jury trial in another city, where the jury found him guilty. I ordered a pre-sentence report and a sex-abuse evaluation to be completed by the experts who author such things. At sentencing, back in my makeshift courtroom, I listened to the arguments of the attorneys as to why I should or shouldn't follow the sentence recommended by the evaluators: prison.

As I explained why I was following the recommendation, the defendant's eyes got big, and then he seemed to tune me out. When I'd finished sentencing him to five-to-life, the officers stepped forward to escort him to the transportation van, and he pivoted and ran for the public exit, knocking folding chairs out of the way as he went. My bailiff, an older, portly man, froze in fear. The two transportation officers, as well as cops waiting in the courtroom for unrelated cases, tackled the defendant. It took five of them to subdue him.

You need to know the whole story behind a case or a person. We can't judge based on appearances (or roles) alone. The defendant probably thought he knew me from how I presented myself on the basketball court; likewise, I thought I knew him from the same arena. But in a different venue, neither of us was prepared for what we found. The defendant and I were shocked to learn who the other was and what he was capable of doing.

I'd never had that happen before, and it hasn't happened since. I'm convinced it wasn't just a reaction to the sentence—he'd been provided a copy of the pre-sentence report recommendations ahead of time. It was the setting and lack of trappings that led to the attempted escape. The place just looked and felt like a house of cards that could be blown over— bolting was certainly at least worth a try. There also may have been a part of him that still thought of me as the guy on the basketball court. He remembered being able to take me off the dribble any time he wanted and thought he had a chance because of our history together. He remembered addressing me as, "Hey, you," rather than, "Your Honor."

Can you Trust the Man in Black?

I'm not opposed to *all* things thespian. I'd just rather be sitting with the audience. And like most people who make their living dispensing justice and mercy, *Les Misérables* is hands down my favorite musical. Clichéd, I know, but there you have it. Among other things, the play's about decency and overcoming the odds. And it's about justice, of course. Right up my alley. I've seen the production probably half a dozen times over the years. The first time I saw it, I was sitting by my wife and watching that jerk cop Javert chase world-class good-guy Jean Valjean all over the stage just for lifting a loaf of bread *decades* earlier. While Javert was yammering on and on about how he brings order and light to the darkness, I leaned over to Arlene and said, "This isn't good!"

"Yes, it is!" she said, meaning the acting.

"No, not that. I mean, I'm sitting here identifying with the villain all dressed in black. You know, what Javert just sang about, 'Those who falter and those who fall must pay the price!'[1] That's pretty much what I'm saying every time I sentence someone!"

"Hmm," she said, the way you would when you're ignoring a kindergartner who's all wound up about Dora's latest encounter at Crocodile Lake.

"But I'm more enlightened than he is," I scoffed. "Stealing a loaf of bread only gets you a $150 fine in my court!"

That's when the people in front and behind us turned and said, "SHHH!"

Epiphanies can arrive at the most inconvenient times.

In a courtroom, as on a stage, the props and the scenery set the framework of where we are. If the props and scenery don't look right, people get confused. If the actors aren't dressed appropriately, they can't command the respect they deserve. The uniforms are important. Otherwise, everyone plays the same role, and you have anarchy. If forty-two thousand fans are at a game, and the pitch is on the outside corner of the plate, according to the Giants fans, it's a ball, and the Dodgers fans scream it is a strike. It's called one or the other. Half cheer, half boo, but all are stuck with the call. Why? Because one guy out of forty-two thousand said so. The one wearing black clothes who was standing right behind home plate, a foot behind the catcher. That's it, and the game moves on.

NOTES

1.   Herbert Kretzmer and Alain Boublil, "Stars," *Les Misérables*, recorded 1986, soundtrack.

5 Where Perry Mason Got It Wrong

I've never been a fan of *Perry Mason,* but I realize I'm in the minority. I know lots of attorneys and judges, most of whom are smarter than me, who watched that show as kids and swear it was the spark that got them headed toward a legal career. Even Supreme Court Justice Sonia Sotomayor spoke of just that in her confirmation hearings. Not so with me. I found the show both predictable and unbelievable— even before I became an attorney. In one criminal case after another, the defendant is innocent and the murderer pops out of his seat like scorched toast and declares his guilt.

Maybe I'd feel differently if Perry had been a part of my youth, but I never saw the show during its heyday. We didn't have a television set. Not because of poverty, mind you, but because my parents—both educators—felt that it would be better if we children did the dishes, practiced the piano, and read.

I see their point now, but I didn't then. I wanted to watch cartoons like everyone else and I wasn't going to just sit there and do nothing about it. So I'd show up at friends' houses on Saturday mornings wondering what time *Mighty Mouse* started.

"Hi, Bobby. I'd let you in, but Rex isn't awake yet," Mrs. Osborne would say, and I'd come back a half hour later, figuring if it didn't start at 7:30, then it must start at 8:00. I quickly learned that mothers had more patience than fathers when it came to dealing with annoying grade-school neighbors. Fathers sent me away. Mothers at least let me in, showing me where to sit until my friend woke up. I was happy to do this no matter how long it took.

In later years, I expanded my parasitic viewing into the afternoon—TV-watching fairness being a twenty-four hour proposition. After school, my friends and I would play one kind of ball or another until the serial shows cranked up, and then we'd stay in front of the tube until the plug was pulled.

"Bobby, your mother just called, and said it was time to come home."

"But *The Lone Ranger* just started," my friend and I would say in unison.

"She said if you aren't home in five minutes, you'll be grounded."

I'd hustle home, wondering how my parents could embarrass our whole family like this.

I tried to get them to buy a TV, using a variety of different tacks—relentless pleading being employed most often—but they resisted.

"I feel sorry for Elaine," I confided to my mother one night as we were pulling the dishes from the drainer, hand-drying them, and placing them in the cupboard. Elaine was my eight-year-old sister and, as the youngest and the only girl, the apple of my mother's eye.

"Why?"

"Other kids are teasing her at recess."

"What did they say?" she asked patiently. She had this way of putting down the dish towel and turning to me that told me, *This had better be good.*

"They made fun of her because she didn't know what happened on *Bonanza* on Sunday!"

Heartless to the core, she smiled and walked off. "You finish up here. I'll go see if she's okay now."

Why did I say Bonanza? Elaine didn't give a crap about *Bonanza!* By now she and mom would be laughing at me upstairs in her bedroom.

Just like prohibition drove poor Al Capone into a life of crime bootlegging booze, my parents' TV prohibition turned a pure child into a con man. Of necessity, by the time I was in junior high, I had learned the effectiveness of bait-and-switch tactics.

"Can I go to Ronnie's and study for our history test?" I'd say, holding up my textbook.

"Sure," Mom would say, and I'd be off to study history—for five minutes. And then I'd watch *The Fugitive.* It was a gambit that worked well so long as I didn't overplay it.

Eventually my parents gave in and bought a television set in 1965. They never said why. Maybe it was because they wanted to watch TV themselves. After all, when the Beatles made their nationally publicized appearance on *The Ed Sullivan Show* in 1964, a friend's parents invited our family to see the show, which we gladly did. We even cut Sunday dinner short in order to arrive in time.

"I don't see what the big deal is," said our fathers.

"He's supposed to be the cute one," said my friend's mother, pointing at Paul McCartney. We all agreed with her and with the fact that Ringo was, indeed, homely, but none of us could understand the frenzied screaming by the girls in the audience. How could they be attracted to grown men with the same haircut as half the five-year-old girls in our neighborhood? The whole thing was mesmerizing, and as we watched and compared notes and generally had a wonderful time, we felt connected to what the rest of the country and *LIFE* magazine were talking about. As we walked home, my parents must have felt just a tad bit exposed, an obvious "kick me" sign slapped on their backs reading: *Our high standards don't allow for a television, but we're not above watching yours.*

At least that's my take, but a more likely explanation is my parents were finally embarrassed enough over my begging for entertainment food scraps up and down the street that they caved and bought me my own "idiot box."

When my son was in high school, his civics class watched law and motion hearings for an hour in my court. It was a proud moment for me. At home that night, I asked him what the class thought. "It was cool," he said and changed the subject. Unconvinced, I asked, "What aren't you saying?"

"Well, it's important and everything, but it just isn't as interesting as *Law and Order.*"

Damned television! I thought. *Sam Waterston is making me look bad.*

Normally I avoid movies and television shows involving courtroom activities. For one thing, it reminds me of work. For another, I can't help but blurt out, "Defendants don't give closing arguments at arraignment!" Or, "No judge would let an attorney talk to him like that!" or some other verbal flagging of an obvious violation of the Rules of Criminal Procedure, and then my family asks if I would please leave the room.

Not being capable of leaving well enough alone, I watched a couple of episodes of *Law and Order,* and I found it was well written, well acted, and fast paced. Some of the courtroom stuff was ridiculously off base, but it *was* more interesting than my court: crimes were committed, cases solved, and decisions reached by the jury *all in less than an hour*. There is no crime—so to speak—in watching a show like that. Just don't view it as a sneak peek at the criminal justice system, because it's not. As the show itself says in the opening graphic: "This story is fictional. No actual person or event is depicted."

That's a point that often gets lost on viewers. Sometimes misconceptions acquired from watching TV can gum up the proceedings in real cases. Like the felony date-rape case I had a few years ago.

The jury was deliberating and after an hour or two, the bailiff came to my chambers. "The jury has a question they want to ask you."

"Have them put it in writing and tell the attorneys we're reconvening to address the question."

I took the bench and stated for the record what had happened. "Do you have the written question?"

"Yes," he said, handing me a folded-over piece of paper from a yellow legal pad.

Why didn't the police take fingerprints at the crime scene, and why wasn't there any DNA evidence given to us?

Dumbfounded, I put the paper down and looked to the attorneys for help understanding these absurd questions, given that fingerprints wouldn't have helped either side in this case.

They looked as confused as I was and then the defense attorney started laughing. "They've been watching too much *CSI*!" he said.

Ah, yes. We all shook our heads. He'd nailed the problem. *CSI*: where everything hinges on scientific evidence and police departments have unlimited budgets to hire brilliant scientists and the latest expensive equipment. Problem is, none of it is needed in many cases, especially this one.

In our case, a coed and a male college student met at a party. They only knew each other very casually before the night in question. Then they retired to the defendant's bedroom, where they had sex. Everyone agreed on those facts. Where the two sides differed was how the sex occurred. The defendant said the sex was consensual. The coed said she participated in kissing, and then the defendant put a pillow over her mouth so she could only breathe through her nose, said if she made any noise he would "hurt her real bad," and raped her. Like all date rape cases, the jury had a tough decision to make: do you believe the defendant, or do you believe the alleged victim? There were no tie-breaking third party witnesses, and certainly no scientific evidence that would tilt the scales for the jury. Fingerprints and DNA evidence would only show that the defendant was there and had sex—evidence that was agreed to by both sides.

"Any objections to me just writing, 'You must decide this case on the evidence presented during the trial,' without editorializing any further?" I asked the attorneys.

Both said that was fine with them.

And let me say this: sometimes you read about a prosecutor having a ninety-something percent conviction rate. If you have that kind of a winning percentage, you are only going to trial on slam-dunk cases. Date rape cases don't fit into that category. Sure, you should, and must, screen the cases and only go to trial with believable victims that tell a consistent, compelling story. But even with that, unfortunately, many date-rape cases boil down to a he-said, she-said case. And with the burden of proof being "beyond a reasonable doubt," you are going to lose some cases. So why try them at all? Because if you never try them, you have just de facto legalized date rape on your campus or in your community. Refusing to try date rape cases sends the abhorrent message: "Have at it boys, because I don't want my stats harmed."

Go ahead and enjoy the original *CSI* set just down the road from me in Las Vegas, or *CSI: Miami*, *CSI: NY*, and the other proliferating police-prosecutorial courtroom drama TV shows, and enjoy them for what they are: entertainment. Just don't bring the TV mind-set into the real courtroom. Not every case hinges on scientific evidence, not every defendant is innocent, not every private investigator is flawed but brilliant, and not every warden is evil.

Not that crime shows can't do a little educating of the lay public once in a while. For example, anyone who watches them knows what his or her Miranda rights are without having to actually read *Miranda v. Arizona*. I once had a misdemeanant defendant interrupt me when I said he had the right to remain silent, explaining to me with exasperation, "I know what my rights are!" Several people there with citations nodded to me from the audience.

But often people *don't* understand the connection between their rights and how it applies to their case. At least once a month I'll get someone who says, "They didn't read me my rights. I think the case should be thrown out."

"Did you confess to anything?"

"No."

"Then there's no confession to be thrown out. If you want to have a trial, just plead not guilty, and I'll see what the evidence is, but I'm not throwing it out now."

As a judge, I honestly believe *Perry Mason* did a disservice to the public—and continues to do so through present-day reruns. It misleads viewers about courtroom realities, in particular in the areas of the cross examination of witnesses and confessions, not to mention the fantasy that one hundred percent of defendants are innocent. After sampling a few *Perry Mason* reruns, I knew that, if charged with a crime I didn't commit (or one I *did* commit, for that matter), all I'd have to do was hire Perry. It quickly became apparent that the answer to "Whodunit?" was always, "Notthedefendant."

All across the land, traffic court defendants, small-claims litigants, and way too many lawyers who should know better think that if you truly believe in your cause and aggressively cross-examine long enough, an opposing witness will ultimately snap-to and be your puppet. After all, it works for Perry Mason.

The recalcitrant cop will say, "By golly, you're right. The light *was* green."

The landlord will say, "Why yes, now that you insist upon it, I reverse my testimony. You *did* pay the March rent!"

So off they go, asking question after question, imagining that they are at a *Perry Mason* Fantasy Camp, pacing the courtroom and stridently challenging witnesses, fruitlessly grinding on and on.

Rather than converting an opposing witness to the cross-examiner's cause, what happens over and over again is that the questioner has an opposing witness repeat damaging testimony, arguing with him as he goes along. The more damaging the testimony, the more times it is repeated, and the angrier and less effective the questioner becomes.

Once agitated and rolling in full-Mason mode, cross-examiners just can't stop themselves. They ask questions that end up letting the adverse witness clear up any inconsistencies, rather than tactically saving those inconsistencies for exposure during closing argument. Sure, you can—and should—do some damage to opposing witnesses with carefully thought-out and carefully worded questions, but you have to know when to stop.

I once had a serious domestic-violence case in which the victim was hospitalized from the attack. The defense attorney had done a good job challenging a prosecution witness who lived in an apartment below that of the victim and her husband and who claimed to know what had happened upstairs. Toward the end of his cross-examination, the attorney asked the witness, "Did you ever see the defendant hit his wife?"

"No."

"In fact, you didn't actually *see* anything that took place, did you?"

"No."

"And you couldn't make out any words that were being said upstairs, could you?"

"No."

The defense attorney should have stopped there and pounded those points home in closing argument. But there was blood in the water, and so he asked one more question.

"So how can you claim my client hurt his wife if you didn't see or hear *anything*?"

The witness spoke as fast as he could to get his message out: "Because they were screaming at each other, and then there was a loud thump on the ceiling, and I never heard her voice again. And when the ambulance guys carried her out the front door on a stretcher, he was looking down at her and grinning."

Whoops. Case over. I know, because there was no jury on this one.

This isn't a unique story. Ask any experienced trial judge or attorney and he'll have a similar tale to tell.

Cross-examination is a tough thing to do well, and I was certainly no master at it. Sometimes the best thing is to ask no questions, especially if the witness hasn't really harmed your case. But if you must ask, don't expect Perry results.

And confessions? I have never had someone in my court confess to a murder—or any other crime for that matter—due to vigorous cross-examination.

Not that courtrooms lack drama or an occasional unexpected twist.

I was a greenhorn judge, just six weeks on the bench in 1987, when I had my first encounter with a defendant charged in a death penalty case. He was brought into my courtroom for his first appearance, where he was provided a written copy of the charges against him. Recently released from the Nevada state penitentiary, the defendant had been arrested in Utah and charged with capital homicide.

Right out of the chute, I made a rookie error—and he schooled me. After I called his case, he continued to slouch and stare at the wall on his left as if I didn't exist, and he didn't have a care in the world. He was also still wearing the dark sunglasses I had overheard his attorney tell him to remove.

In my sternest voice, I said, "Take off those sunglasses!" When he turned to look at me, I fixed him with what I hoped was a withering glare. A muscular young man, with thick black hair, he did nothing for a couple of seconds; then he laughed and tossed the glasses on the table in disgust and stared at me. I blinked—and instantly knew two things: first, someone facing the death penalty isn't going to be scared by a judge giving him a few days jail for contempt of court (what was I *thinking*?), and second, this guy had the darkest and most soulless eyes I had ever looked into. He totally unnerved me.

The following Sunday, I received the weekly call from the sergeant at the jail, who also served as a transportation officer bringing inmates to my court. He read the usual collection of probable-cause statements concerning that weekend's arrests, and I fixed bail according to the severity of the crime. Then, as always, he asked what football game I was watching, what the score was, and good-naturedly reminded me that I had a "cushy" job.

Curious to see if I had imagined things earlier that week, I asked him if he had ever looked hard into the defendant's eyes.

After a short pause, he said, "Yeah. And I know what you mean."

It's not a look I've seen since.

The murder confession occurred the second time I met the defendant. I was conducting the preliminary hearing, where the prosecution has to present just enough evidence to establish that there is probable cause to believe the charged offense occurred, and was committed by the defendant. (In laymen's terms—it's more likely than not that the defendant did it.) In short, should this guy have to stand trial?

During direct examination, the investigating officer presented evidence that a man from California had been traveling through Utah on his way to another state to look for work when he had been stabbed to death. His body had been dumped off the side of I-15 like so much litter tossed from a car, where it was found a few days later. (In my mind, I can still see the black-and-white autopsy photos: the fatal stab wounds here and there in his torso, his body bloated by the summer heat.) The prosecution's theory was that the victim picked up a hitchhiker, the defendant, who had robbed and murdered him. The officer testified that the defendant had been found in possession of the victim's credit cards and clothes, some of which had blood on them.

The victim's ex-wife then took the stand to verify ownership of the clothing. The prosecution laid the foundation for her identification of the clothing. "While I can't say definitively that this was Robert's red shirt," she'd testified, "or that this was his pair of blue jeans, I *can* say that they are the size he wore, and I have seen him wearing clothes just like these."

She held up under the emotional strain of identifying item after item, until she got to the underwear. When the prosecutor handed her a pair of boxer shorts—dark blue, if I remember correctly—she hesitatingly accepted the shorts, and then, as if her arm suddenly had no muscles, her hand dropped to her lap. Her shoulders sagged, and she began to cry.

As the prosecutor approached, asking if she wanted a drink of water or a tissue, there was a commotion over at the defense table. I looked at the defense attorney, a long-time colleague and now fellow judge, Jim Shumate. He was huddled with his client, the two engaged in an earnest and animated discussion. I could not hear what they were saying, nor did I want to, but I did see some emphatic negative head-shaking from Jim.

Finally, he rose and addressed the court. "Your Honor, my client wants to do something against my advice, and I want to speak with him privately."

I told them to take whatever time they needed and recessed the case. A long time later I reentered the courtroom. Both sides addressed the court and made a record of the fact that the defendant wanted to end the preliminary hearing and plead guilty to the murder, straight up, all against the advice of counsel.

I was never told why the defendant demanded the right to change his plea right then and there in the preliminary hearing. But I've always suspected that, in fact, somewhere behind those foreboding eyes was a person who couldn't bear to see the results of what he had done nor further hear the anguish of those left behind.

In *Perry Mason*, the defendant is always innocent. In *Perry Mason* someone else always declares his guilt. In *Perry Mason*, Perry and his cohorts, Della Street and Paul Drake, all share a chuckle in the final scene at what jolly fun it has been. Not so in real life. The defendant was guilty. The defendant admitted it. Several members of the jury openly wept when their unanimous verdict was read, and on October 15, 1999, Joseph Mitchell Parsons received a lethal injection—the last person executed in the state of Utah in the twentieth century.

6 Pristine Parks and Public Offenses

I grew up listening to those Standard Oil broadcasts about national parks that encouraged people to buy their gas and travel around the country taking in the sights. My fourth-grade teacher would interrupt rote-memorization of multiplication tables—or whatever—and we'd lay down our pencils, rest our heads on the desk, and be transported by stories about glaciers and buffalo and white-hot geysers spewing out water so hot that they would *kill* you in two seconds if you fell in and . . . well, places far away from where we sat trying to ignore the lingering odor from the rug right behind us where Sheldon Stephens threw up twice in one year and they *still* couldn't seem to get the smell out.

I was twelve years old when my Boy Scout troop convoyed in pickups and faux-wood-paneled station wagons to the North Rim of the Grand Canyon. We arrived at sunset, set up camp, messed around, argued about who would sleep where, and generally got on our scoutmaster's nerves. Then, almost as an afterthought, we asked the scoutmaster where the canyon was. "About fifty yards that way," he said, nodding his head wearily its direction.

Being the fools that we were, three of us raced each other up a rise, sliding to a stop mere feet from the edge of a sheer cliff. And what I saw literally took my breath away—the *only* time I recall that happening. We all stood there dumbstruck, the vast expanse spread out below and in front of us in a muted glow: a layered rainbow of ocher, vermillion, and sienna limestone, sandstone, and shale formations marching down to the jagged river gorge, still visible in the fading light. After a minute or two, we walked back to our camp in reverent silence. Maybe someone whispered, "Wow," maybe not. But it's what we felt.

The twenty-four mile forced march from the North Rim to the South Rim began the next morning. At the first rest stop, just a couple of miles down Bright Angel Trail, Gordon Topham, who'd been criticized by the scoutmaster for bringing a backpack that weighed in as too heavy, opened it up and offered to sell nickel candy bars for a quarter. No one bought anything because they thought it was a dirty trick. Really unfair. Not me. I was mad at myself for not thinking of the idea first.

When we were about nine, my best friend Clyde and I would walk to Park 'N Shop, buy Tootsie Roll Pops and crappy small candy bars for two cents each, walk home, tape nickel price tags on them, and lay them out in a row on a card table in front of his house. Sometimes kids bought them, and sometimes they didn't. When they didn't, we happily ate our inventory. I thought of that as I looked at Gordon's huge stash and hoped he'd have a bad stomachache soon. But he sold it all by dinnertime. He had money, the other Scouts had candy, and I didn't have either. Dumb, dumb, dumb!

After this lesson in capitalism, we trudged down to the Colorado River, then up to the South Rim, and—camping at Cottonwood, Phantom Ranch, and Indian Gardens—we learned the things all Boy Scouts learn. Kenyon Thompson, hiking right in front of me, learned that if you cinch the straps of your backpack too tight on your shoulders, it restricts the blood flow and you will pass out and fall to the ground like a lifeless duffle bag. This shook me up because Kenyon was much stronger than I was. I mean, sheesh—*I* didn't work in my dad's brickyard every day.

We also learned universal truths: water can be the best drink you've ever had, popping blisters is only neat when it involves someone else's foot, nothing looks pretty when it's ninety degrees, and walking in sand is a lot more work than walking on pavement. Finally, we learned that after you pull your dinner from the fire—an aluminum foil-covered concoction of meat, vegetables and potatoes—you'll wish you had *anything* cooked by your mother instead of this half-raw, half-burned glob of crap you just cobbled together. ("Open up the packages and use the foil itself for plates. Ummmmmmmmmmm!" the *Boys' Life* article had gushed.)

For the five-hour drive home after we'd been shuttled back to the North Rim, my friends and I talked the scoutmaster into letting us ride in the back of a pickup instead of crammed like sardines into the tin of the station wagon we had arrived in. It was not just any pickup, mind you, but a modified livestock truck, the bed fortified with tall wooden slats all around to hold in animals—in this case a half-dozen Boy Scouts. All the troop's rolled-up sleeping bags were lobbed up and over the railings, landing every which way in the bed of the truck. Then we scampered up over the slats, and burrowed down into the bags until only our heads were exposed. A late-afternoon summer thundershower had pelted the high, Kaibab Plateau earlier, drawing a strong pine scent from the ponderosa forest.

As the cool night air whipped by, we talked about how tomorrow we would go buy a hamburger and a root beer with crushed ice at the Dairy Freeze, and the food would be *hot* and the drink would be *cold,* and that pretty soon we'd be home and showering off this pungent BO and sleeping on a soft mattress instead of rocks. We also talked about how we'd missed our homes and families and how we'd *never* take them for granted again or tease little brothers. But then we thought about what we'd just said, and laughed because we knew what a pack of liars we were. But we'd seen the best sunset we'd ever see in our lives, and now we had *real* stories to scare the new Tenderfoot-Rank Scouts with—stories of the Grand Canyon Death March. And without saying anything out loud, we felt just a little bit stronger and a little bit older. At least I know I did.

Four years later, I returned to the North Rim, not as a scout, but as an awkward teenager with a summer job. I had wanted to get away from home, stay in a dorm with older (cooler) kids, maybe break out of my shell, and have *an adventure,* and this seemed like the perfect way to pull it off.

It didn't turn out at all the way I'd dreamed. The dishwashing job only paid seventy cents an hour because the lodge provided room and board. Room was two barn-like, depression-era dorms—one for girls, one for boys, four workers to a stall. Board was largely the previous day's unsold specials, like stew made from chicken or steak about to go bad. Not exactly as bad as the fare in *Oliver Twist,* but all of us kitchen swine felt justified in doing a little pilfering from the fresher stock. The hot rolls were easy picking: cram one into your mouth, and chew discretely while you scrub dishes. But beating your coworkers to the fried jumbo shrimp from the bussed plates called for speed and overt ruthlessness.

I swore I'd never eat in a restaurant again after what I saw that summer. Standard practice was to return dropped food to the customer whenever possible. Say, for example, you heard a crash in the dining room, and a minute later a waitress came through the swinging door with the picked-up mess spread out on a tray held level with her shoulder. She'd go over to a serving table, brush off the chicken breast, roll, and cooked carrots, arrange them just-so on a new plate, have the cook spoon on fresh mashed potatoes and gravy (no way to redeem those!) and the new entree would then be whisked out to the appreciative customer.

As to the social life, well . . . I was the only sixteen-year-old there, and I hadn't gone through puberty: five foot three, with a voice that hadn't even started to crack yet. At night when we were talking in our bunk beds, someone passing in the hall would throw open our door, turn on the lights, and yell, "Who's got a girl in his bed?" pause a second, then add, "Oh yeah—it's just Braithwaite!" It was a gag that never got old. For them.

Unlike my first visit as a scout, I didn't even enjoy the scenery. No one did. There it was, just a few steps away from the lodge, and after a while we didn't even look. Some of the employees even called it "the hole." The cool college kids weren't much interested in hanging out with the half-dozen high schoolers. *Especially* the coeds. Apparently if you're a nerdy geek at home, you don't transform into an alluring character just because you change your address. Who knew?

I wanted to quit, but my mother said, "Nope, if you quit at this, you'll quit at other challenging things in life, so you're staying. It will be a good experience." (I *hated* that phrase. *It's not a good experience*, I thought. *It's a* bad *experience. You can make me stay, but you can't make me buy into your ridiculous parenting phrases.*) Though she never elaborated, I understood her meaning by the time I hit basic training at Fort Campbell, Kentucky, three years later. When things got bad and guys started going AWOL, I didn't think of running for even a second. Those of us who stayed were having a *good experience*: enduring a perfectly crappy time because that's what you've got to do and learning what you can from having made a bad decision that got you where you are.

Nowadays, I return to Grand Canyon and other national parks as an adult. My bad experiences at the Grand Canyon were softened and forgotten—except as footnotes—as I aged. I matured, married, and the jaw-dropping memory of my first encounter with the Canyon brought me back, family in tow. I continue to want to share the parks with children and grandchildren.

With that in mind, I asked my daughter's permission to take my oldest grandkid on a park experience and spend time strengthening our bond. Rather than heading for a park near me, I thought we'd go somewhere that might be more tailor-made for this eight-year-old.

Like most little kids, Calvin was nuts about dinosaurs, so I was taking him to Dinosaur National Monument in northwestern Utah. He didn't just wear Brachiosaurus briefs, and Triceratops T-shirts, he had books crammed with facts on the Jurassic beasts. I asked him what his favorite was, and he said, "The Utahraptor."

"Because of its name?"

"Yes, and because it's the biggest raptor ever—like six feet tall! And it hunts in packs. My second favorite is Ceratosaurus; it has horns and is tall."

From my home, I drove three hours up I-15, threw his backpack in the car, made sure he was belted in, and trundled east on Highway 40. Calvin is a wiry kid, a little below average height, and he skims around a playground like a water bug, always keeping just out of reach when playing tag. He has an intense intelligence about him—an effect that is no doubt heightened by his Harry Potter glasses.

Not being a dummy on how to win the hearts of children, I stopped forty minutes into the drive at Heber City and asked him if he wanted a milkshake. "Yes!" he said. He read the drive-thru menu at the Dairy Keen and said, "I'd like to try marshmallow."

"Cool!" I said. "That was my favorite milkshake when I was your age, except I liked raspberry syrup mixed in too—want to try it?"

"Nope, just marshmallow," he said.

Obviously, the kid hadn't inherited my sophisticated palate. I ordered a caramel cashew milkshake for myself, and we slurped up those shakes until there was nothing left, stopping only occasionally to let the brain-freeze headaches recede a tad. It was a bit porcine, but so what? This was a *guy* trip.

Then we continued east through the high, bleak desert and across the Uintah Basin for two and a half hours. We didn't say much, and were happy as trilobites (before they went extinct in the Permian Period, naturally), because Calvin had a brand-new book on dinosaurs, and I had a football game on satellite radio.

In the Braithwaite family, this is known as *male bonding*.

It was foggy and cold when we arrived at Dinosaur National Monument. We were the only visitors in the Monument on such a gloomy day. As a result, we received a warm welcome at the Visitor Center and had a personally guided tour of the quarry by a park ranger, a very nice young woman from Florida. It was perfect.

She took us to a two-story building that had been fabricated so that one of the walls was an archeologically excavated flood plain that had been geologically uplifted to a 45-degree angle. This fourth wall displayed exposed thighbones, spines, teeth, skulls, and pretty much every kind of dinosaur body part you could imagine, all separated and resting in their final burial places. The building made it a warm place to be, even as the wind and snow blew around outside.

The ranger used a laser pointer to identify and describe all the things embedded in the wall, highlighting the jaws with serrated teeth and claws for Calvin's nervous pleasure. He was especially impressed with a head and jaw as long as his own body.

"Do you have any Utahraptors?" Calvin asked after all the dinosaurs on the wall were identified.

"No," said the ranger, smiling. "They came here long after these dinosaurs. These are what were trapped in an ocean bed of silt. But you can find them in other parts of the state."

After posing for a picture by the fossilized bones of another dinosaur, Calvin and I said good-bye to the ranger and headed for Vernal where we checked into—what else—the Dinosaur Motel.

The next morning we slept in, ate a hearty breakfast of bacon and eggs, pancakes with syrup, and fresh orange juice, and . . . well, life was good.

We stopped by a new state park dinosaur museum for a quick tour, and I did what any grandparent would do—I bought souvenirs: a new dinosaur T-shirt; a book, *Amazing Dinosaurs: More Feathers, More Claws, Big Horns, Wide Jaws!*; and some dinosaur toys.

As I drove toward Calvin's home, I started to apologize for not having anything to entertain him, but Calvin, genuinely surprised, looked up at me through his glasses and said, "It's okay, Papa. I can just read the comics."

A few weeks later, I got a small booklet from him in the mail. The blank pages had been filled with his second-grade scrawl and hand-drawn pictures about our trip. He'd entitled the work, "I Like it When," because each page started with "I like it when . . ." accompanied by a picture he'd drawn on the opposite page of something we had done or seen. My favorite was, "I like it when we go on trips" with a drawing of us as stick figures, sitting in my pickup admiring what was probably intended to be a Monoclonius, but which looked more like a cross between a turtle and a unicorn. Clearly he had inherited my artistic ability and not his art-professor grandmother's.

I was blown away when I got the book. Obviously his mother had helped by buying the book and shipping it for him, but the writing was all his. He'd loved our trip. He loved me, and he loved Dinosaur National Monument. It's an enjoyable pilgrimage we've repeated since. Some people feel like a visit to a park can be almost like a religious retreat. I feel that way sometimes too. Perhaps it's a religion Calvin will choose to adopt as well.

I'm lucky to have a job where I work to protect national parks the best I can by hearing cases that come up when people visit and use our parks. But, I'm sorry to say, the public interaction with the parks doesn't always go perfectly. It never has.

The National Park Service Organic Act of 1916 is probably not fused into your DNA, but I'm sure you know the general idea, that the fundamental purpose of National Parks is to "conserve the scenery and the natural and historic objects and the wild life therein and to provide for the enjoyment of the same in such manner and by such means as will leave them unimpaired (emphasis added) for the enjoyment of future generations."[1]

Does that sum it up or what? Well, there's that word, *unimpaired*. To me, it's straightforward. But opinions differ. There have been conflicts about how the parks are to be run, and how to interpret that word *unimpaired* since day one.

For example, John Muir, the original champion of Yosemite—who could cover fifty miles of strenuous up-and-down hiking on foot in two days with only a few pounds of crackers, oatmeal, and tea, all while "contemplating the life of a raindrop," and "witnessing the work and presence of God"[2]—wanted to keep the entire Yosemite tract as pristine as possible. The city of San Francisco thought having a Yosemite National Park was all well and good, but its leaders figured one of its most spectacular sites— the Hetch Hetchy Valley—should be under water, the better to fill the city pipes. San Francisco prevailed with the US Congress, and—dunk— no more Hetch Hetchy Valley.

The conflict between those who want the land to stay as is and those who see the land as a resource and want to harvest the minerals, lumber, animals, and what have you has been a constant in our nation's history.

Sometimes the variance even plays out within a single person over a lifetime. Teddy Roosevelt, lauded as a champion of conservation—and rightfully so—didn't start out that way. As a twenty-four-year-old, he heard that the buffalo on the western plains were surely on the verge of extinction. His response? He rushed to North Dakota to what is now Teddy Roosevelt National Park, so he wouldn't be denied the chance to kill one. This he did, cutting the bull's head off and mounting it on his wall in New York.

Sometimes activities in the parks aren't just a matter of policy debate, they descend into criminal activity. Some crimes, such as poaching, have been, and always will be, illegal, even allowing for a modern twist or two.

Take the case I heard involving the Rocky Mountain bighorn sheep and the ultra-light airplane. A big-game hunter shelled out a bunch of money to a guide to help him bag the sheep. They went to the rugged Waterpocket Fold section of Utah adjacent to Capitol Reef—where, since it's a national park—hunting is illegal. Up in the air goes the quiet plane. Down on the ground, the wildlife roams in natural patterns. The pilot methodically crisscrosses the rugged desert landscape below until he finds a ram, notes its direction of travel, and radios down the GPS coordinates directing the ATV-prowling hunter towards the prey. The process is repeated and fine tuned, the noose tightens, and the sheep is killed. This is hunting? Evolution should have somehow engineered wildlife for predator drones in the sky? What kind of person gets satisfaction from this? It's pretty disgusting on both ends—I mean, at one point; the guide must have loved hunting and had some respect for the animals, right? What happened? And how delusional and insecure does a hunter have to be to feel that this proves anything about his manhood or dominance? Somewhere along the line both have lost touch with reality.

The only wildlife case I recall that documented worse sportsmanship involved a black bear taken in Dixie National Forest. A guide and his son used dogs to track the bear and tree it. The guide left the son with some provisions, a rifle, and the dogs surrounding the tree, drove from Webster's Flat some dozen miles down to Cedar City, and called his client in Las Vegas, who then drove the four hours to Webster's Flat and shot the bear out of the tree. Contrary to what they might tell admirers of the bearskin rug spread out in their den, hunters like that have *cojones* the size of BBs.

Early one autumn evening, my family and I were polishing off a barbecue dinner when the kitchen phone rang. I listened as a ranger from Zion National Park laid out the scenario: four men with brightly-colored parachutes had just sprinted to the edge of the massive, sheer-cliff wall of Mount Kinesava, plunged off, and floated to the valley floor thousands of feet below. The jump was performed in full view of witnesses, including a park employee. Landing on a slope away from roads, they'd strolled down the Chinle Trail, where they were intercepted by a ranger.

BASE jumping—skydiving from a fixed object—is illegal in national parks. The ranger asked if he could search the parachutists' backpacks, and they refused, so the ranger held them while another ranger called me to request a search warrant. I immediately signed and faxed back the warrant, and the ranger found parachutes matching the description given by the park employee.

By the time the jumpers' arraignments rolled around a couple of weeks later, the local prosecutor had researched the case and negotiated a plea agreement with the defendants. As the case was presented to me, it was never really a question of guilt or innocence, just a question of what the sentence should be after the defendants pled guilty. (Free legal tip: If you're going to maintain your innocence, it's a good idea not to film the event, describe your exploits, and post it all on your website where the prosecutor can download it.)

This was *a case of first impression* in my court (a legal term that makes a judge sound way smarter than saying, "Geez—I haven't had a case like this before!"), so the prosecutor called other parks and discovered that the standard sentence at Yosemite National Park, a mecca for BASE jumpers, was $2,000 plus forfeiture of the parachute gear. The prosecutor reported this sentence had become standard in Yosemite owing to the amount of time and personnel involved in dealing with the burgeoning caseload and the aftermath of fatal jumps. BASE jumping is, and always has been, a crime (technically, the charge is, "unlawful delivery by air without a permit"). However, there was a trial period of ninety days in 1980 when the park service said, in effect, "Okay. Let's see if we can work out an understanding where we let you jump but you agree to jump only on certain days, with only X number of jumpers per day, and only when wind conditions are Y and Z." Reportedly, after a couple of days, the jumpers decided rules were inconsistent with the very free-spirit concept of BASE jumping and reverted to all kinds of shenanigans—going off on things like skateboards, stilts, and every other sort of contraption. That was the end of allowed jumping—not that it ended the practice. Jumpers kept plunging, the body count mounted, and the Park Service dealt with the trauma of cleaning up corpses and comforting grieving relatives.

Yosemite has such a high volume of visitors and corresponding criminal caseload that it has a full-time magistrate judge and a six-cell jail in the park. I figured that, given their experience, I'd follow their lead in sentencing. Also, it seemed to me the same crime should have the same penalty no matter where it occurs, and that, frankly, if the same sentence *weren't* adopted at Zion, the park might become the default location by budget-conscious BASE jumpers. *BASE jumping is half price at Zion! Utah, here we come!*

In later research, I found that BASE jumpers are a courageous, dedicated lot who are also blind to irony. In 1999, they staged a public rally in Yosemite to protest the "unjust" park policy of banning jumps. To prove how safe BASE jumping was, they organized a demonstration from the face of 3,200-foot El Capitan cliff. With hundreds of tourists watching, the first three jumpers leapt safely, but the parachute of the fourth did not open, her body pile-driving into the granite shards at the base of El Capitan, thus becoming the sixth BASE jumper to die at Yosemite at the time. She was not a novice mind you, but rather, an experienced stuntwoman who had worked on many Hollywood films, including the forebodingly titled *Terminal Velocity*. Your average person would say the BASE jumpers had proved the Park Service's point: BASE jumping is an activity that is not in line with park values, degrades other people's enjoyment and experience of the park, *and is dangerous*. Not so for the jumping community, who vowed to continue to fight against the "unfair" ban.

Nor (shockingly!) did my sentence put an end to BASE jumping in Zion. Videos pop up all the time on YouTube of unidentified jumpers leaping off Observation Point, Scout Lookout, and other peaks to say, "That's just backdrop—look at *me!*"

BASE jumping, like other forms of behavior in the parks, betrays a kind of arrogance, the assumption that the individual is bigger than, and better than, the surroundings. The BASE jumping defendants saw the whole thing as an unfair infringement of their free will. This issue of free will being unfairly curtailed arises frequently in criminal cases, yet many defendants think it is unique to them and their circumstances.

Take scoutmasters who bring fifty scouts to hike in Zion without doing research, find out when they arrive that the maximum size at their camp site is twenty-five scouts, and say, "No problem, we are now two groups of twenty-five. We'll camp here, and you guys move that way a little." Then they're outraged when the ranger doesn't agree with the math; they're positive the constitutional rights of the Boy Scouts of America are being infringed. Or there's the local resident arrested for cutting wood on government land without a permit who wants the case thrown out because his family "has been doing this for generations!"

Or . . . well, the list is endless, because every law bans something that someone *really wants to do*. The park has become about *them* and what they need, rather than appreciating and maintaining what is there. They don't see that if a camping area is continually pounded by too many people, the vegetation is trampled, refuse and waste accumulates, and the net effect over time is an inevitable degradation of the pristine location. This little piece of Eden begins to stink. One oversized group doesn't cause it—it's a cumulative result. Parks exist for the community, and allowing people full rein of their individual rights would then abrogate the rights of the community.

Consider the case of the nature photographer who took his students to the iconic Delicate Arch in Arches National Park and taught them how he uses additional light to better capture and enhance the natural landscape in nighttime photographs. Unfortunately, the artificial light he generated by igniting Duraflame logs scorched and defaced portions of the sandstone below the arch. The artist paid $10,900 in restitution, but the damage was done. Hopefully, he and his students learned the lesson that it's not about them—it's about the park. Your photograph, your huge-group camping trip, your adrenaline rush—none of these is what the park is about.

Recently my wife and I stood in Volcano National Park, mesmerized by what we saw and experienced. Because it is active, the Kīlauea volcano is constantly changing the landscape (at a rate of 800–1300 gallons of lava per second, no less), and its route to the sea varies accordingly.[3] The then-current flow was mostly encapsulated in a cooled lava tube not visible to the naked eye, so the rangers recommended a sunset viewing of the Halema'uma'u Crater from the viewpoint outside the Thomas A. Jaggar Museum. We weren't alone, but it was a reverential group— a congregation of people respectfully watching and stepping aside to share viewpoints. The skies slowly darkened, highlighting the reflective glow cast by the boiling cauldron below into the swirling sulfuric steam ascending to the rim, then dissipating. I was moved by the scene of the earth slowly and inexorably expanding not only the park, but also the island upon which we stood.

The park was what we all came for, needed, and wanted. No sideshows could have improved it. Worship as a communal experience or as a solitary experience in the backcountry is impossible when others take the park as their personal playground or a backdrop for their own self-aggrandizement.

An Edward Abbey quote about humans and hunting sums up my feelings about humans and scenery: "Whenever I see a photograph of some sportsman grinning over his kill, I am always impressed by the striking moral and esthetic superiority of the dead animal to the live one."[4]

El Capitan and Delicate Arch can't be improved upon. Let them be.

A few summers after the bighorn sheep incident in Capitol Reef, a different kind of poaching was systematically denuding wide stretches of fields of wildflowers in Zion National Park's backcountry. The poachers' target was Palmer's penstemon, columns of pale pink flowers shooting three to four feet high out of a sage-green leaf base. The flowers often present a spectacular scene, spread about in bunches across the coral-pink sand floor of Zion National Park. But more important, arguably, than their aesthetic appeal is their job in the ecosystem: penstemon help hold the soil in place.

Over a two-month period, two men walked from plant to plant on Smith Mesa, cramming penstemon seedpods into large feed-sack aprons attached to their waists. Then they dumped the pods onto a tarp and separated out the chaff, eventually filling a dozen large garbage sacks. Their ultimate take was 450 pounds of usable seeds with an estimated commercial sale value of $45,000. Needless to say, if this type of painstaking scouring of seeds continues unchecked, nature's reseeding won't happen, and expansive fields of penstemon on Smith's Mesa will be a thing of the past.

They planned on selling them to a nursery in the small town of Ephraim, Utah, up the road on Highway 89. (Seed vendors buying in bulk have to ensure that collectors have valid permits, but they have no way of knowing where the seeds were actually gathered.)

Both pickers were later found to be illegal aliens living in a makeshift camp, and they were paid fifty dollars a day for working in the ninety-plus degree heat. The person they worked for was never clearly identified nor apprehended.

I took their guilty pleas, ordered a pre-sentence report (which provides details about defendants and their prior arrests, if any), and scheduled sentencing down the road before a district judge in the judicial hierarchy above me. (We crime-fighting magistrate judges have limited powers.) The two defendants were placed on two years' probation, given credit for the three months they'd been waiting in jail, and deported. The confiscated seed would be used for reseeding projects in Zion.

The penstemon case caused me some personal concern later. I have been gradually (my family would say glacially) relandscaping our backyard, replacing the standard suburban non-native shrub and sod setup with drought-resistant native plants. What my dad might have called desert, I've learned to call xeriscaping. I've been visiting nurseries and buying young plants and seed packets for fringe sage, four-wing salt bush, columbine, phlox, and . . . penstemon. Concerned, I went to my den and opened a drawer where I had some recently purchased wildflower seed packets. Had I unintentionally contributed to the degradation of national parks by being a part of a consumer demand for wildflower seeds? I flipped over the seed packet and read the back of it. I saw that the seeds were not from the place in Ephraim, or even from this state—which was a relief, but really no guarantee the seeds hadn't been illegally harvested from some other park or forest.

A more common contact point in the spectrum of conflicts arising between people's behavior and park policies involves smoking pot. One man's view of enjoying a park campground while smoking a joint and "bothering no one" is contradicted by another man's ruined family vacation while sandwiched between slacker camping groups. It isn't a gray area of the law: marijuana use in parks is illegal and will get you arrested. But legal constraints regarding marijuana have lessened recently in America, and as a result, society's changing mores show up in the parks. Many see a turning point in the adoption of Proposition 215 in California, the so-called "medicinal marijuana law." The law is fairly straight-forward, if just a tad open-ended in defining who is exempt from criminal punishment, namely *"seriously ill Californians . . .* whose health would benefit from the use of marijuana in the treatment of cancer, AIDS, chronic pain, . . . *or any other illness"* (emphasis added).[5]

Since the law was passed, many a Californian has risen from his deathbed to smoke some pot while taking in the wonders of spectacular Southern Utah. South Campground in Zion National Park can be a virtual sick bay for Californians on weekends. Retirees in Winnebagos, young people in tents, and especially twenty- and thirty-somethings who have just finished the demanding, iconic Zion hikes down the Virgin River Narrows or up and out on Angel's Landing all grouse about being hassled when they have *this prescription!* I sometimes wonder if there is anyone left in the ICU facilities back home.

After Proposition 215 was passed, one of its authors was arrested with felony possession of marijuana in a Cedar City Motel 6. His defense was that he could somehow bring a California law with him to Utah and have it apply here. Other defendants over the years have suffered from the same belief, waving their prescriptions in court like get-out-of-jail-free cards. Unfortunately, you can't take your home-state law with you as you travel to the other forty-nine states. (*But, Your Honor—prostitution is legal in Tonopah, Nevada!*)

But there's a more insidious drug problem in the parks and on other public lands: when they are used for criminal enterprises. Consider these news reports:

- *National Geographic News*, January 13, 2003. "In August, a park ranger, 28-year-old Kris Eggle, was killed while helping Border Patrol agents catch two men suspected by Mexican officials in a drug-related quadruple murder." The hit men were using the park as a drug corridor.[6]
- *San Francisco Chronicle*, November 18, 2005. "National Parks' Pot Farms Blamed on Cartels/Mexican drug lords find it easier to grow in state than import." Forty-four thousand pot plants were removed from Sequoia National Park and ten thousand plants from Yosemite National Park. The grows were protected by booby traps and guards carrying AK-47s.[7]

- *Outside Magazine*, June 2012. "Weed Whackers. Things have gotten crazy violent in the dark, dense forests of California's Mendocino County, where pot growers from Mexico run elaborate plantations they'll defend to the death. Damon Tabor saddles up with Sheriff Tim Allman, head of a helicopter-riding, rifle-toting paramilitary strike force determined to take back the woods."[8]

Marijuana farms are destructive. Growers clear trees, dig ditches, and install extensive plastic tubing drip systems. Vats of fertilizer and banned pesticides poison native species and watersheds. Needless to say, the growers don't clean up any of it when they walk away. Their operations are ripe for violence since their grows are guarded by sentries armed with loaded assault rifles. And it's not just marijuana operations. During a three-year stretch early in the 2000s, 192 meth labs were dismantled in Missouri's Mark Twain National Forest.

One summer afternoon, I sat at my kitchen table reading a complaint regarding a grow site stumbled upon by a hunter. A paragraph concerned me, so I posed the obvious question to the Drug Enforcement Administration agent patiently watching me read. "Sooner or later some innocent hiker or hunter is going to stumble into one of these armed operations and get blown away, right?"

He literally squirmed in his seat and hesitated before answering. "You're probably right, but some of the guys we picked up last year are talking now, and they say their orders are basically threefold: one, if the site is spotted by a hiker, they're to walk off and hide; two, that if it's law enforcement they're to drop their weapons and run 'cause they know we can't shoot 'em; and three, shoot it out if it's another drug operation."

"Another drug operation?"

"Yeah. They steal from each other. *That's* why they have armed lookouts."

This particular grow was situated in the Pine Valley Wilderness Area, perched on a ten-thousand-foot mountain island rising out of the desert. It's a gorgeous place I've visited both on foot and on horseback. The evergreen and aspen forests are frequently broken up with lush meadows, and from its eastern rim you can look into portions of Zion National Park to the east. The Forest Service supervises the wilderness in addition to the national forest that spills over the wilderness boundary and down the steep slopes of the Pine Valley Mountains. The remoteness and growing capacity of the area has not escaped the notice of marijuana growers.

An archery hunter with a valid mule deer tag had followed an old game trail up the east fork of Water Canyon. Eventually he came upon a fertilizer bag beside the path, and then rows of marijuana plants serviced by an intact drip irrigation system. Realizing what he'd discovered, he wisely retreated with his over-matched bow and arrow and informed authorities. This being the twenty-first century, he also provided exact coordinates for the site from his GPS receiver.

Local, state, and federal officers coordinated a raid on the site, advancing by foot, vehicle and helicopter. Nine suspects were captured. An unknown number escaped. An assortment of loaded handguns and assault rifles were found in the camp or where they'd been dropped along the trail as the growers fled.

"With all that manpower and equipment, how did people get away?" I later asked the agent.

"The forests are thick, and they know all the trails and 'rabbit holes.' Plus they're younger than us, and we're carrying a lot of gear—body armor, weapons, belts." He shrugged. "All they've got to do is run."

Of the nine suspects caught, three were illegal aliens, and two of the US citizens were alleged gang members. When they were brought to court, some sat stiffly in their chairs, obviously scared, staring unblinking at me or the interpreter, depending on which of us was speaking. Others slouched as if they'd been poured into their chairs, eyelids at half-mast, affecting a practiced nonchalance that said, "This is nothing. Just say your bullshit so we can go back to jail." Those with tattoos spreading out from under their jump suits fell into the latter category.

Most listed minimum wage jobs such as landscaping aide, tire shop employee, and day laborer. The single defendant with enough money to hire an attorney was a US citizen, said he owned two mortgage-free homes in Las Vegas, and said that he had an average annual income of $175,000. He also had active arrest warrants out of Nevada for two murders. Judges aren't supposed to jump to conclusions, but I think I can guess who might have been in charge.

These grows are a major problem. In four counties in southwestern Utah in 2010, marijuana grows were found at seventeen locations on national forest, BLM, and national park lands. In all, over one hundred thousand plants with a value exceeding $215 million were eradicated.

Law enforcement usually says the grows are operated by Mexican drug cartels, and maybe they are. I've just never had a case come through that proved that. Some say that they are actually run by small, US-based Mexican drug gangs. Either way, the result is the same. It's estimated the average taxpayer cost to clean up a grow site is $15,000. And the violence is escalating, with two Native Americans on the tribe's reservation shot to death by pot growers in 2006, and at least three growers shot to death by deputies in California.

Not all raids on grow sites are successful. Sometimes the growers find out the cops are on to them and abandon the sites days—or even hours—before a raid. And growers are getting bolder. At one abandoned grow site near Capitol Reef, they took the time to leave behind a large, hand-written sign thumbing their nose at law enforcement: "Welcome to Marijuana Ranch. 19-07-2010. US—Army!"

When I asked the DEA agent what was with the Army reference, he said, "In Mexico, they fight the Mexican army. I guess that's who they think we are."

Let me add that professionals don't have a monopoly on illegal drug activities on federal land. The Internet is replete with websites and chat rooms about how and where to grow your own pot. In 2006, *Cannabis Culture Magazine* even provided an article by an author calling himself "Boy Scout," entitled, "How to Grow in Forests and Parks," complete with how-to-do-it details and photographs. (Sample entry: "You need to locate a relatively level spot near a creek. But not too close, as you have to account for the bushwhackers traversing the stream in pursuit of happiness!")[9]

The incentives for those who want to grow are significant. It's estimated that a medium-sized grow of ten thousand plants will gross $25 million, which means that this fight is far from over.

When I get a bit down about the future of public lands and national parks, a great kid like Calvin can help me keep things in perspective. When he's engaged with dinosaurs, be it reading a detailed book about them, or acting out life-and-death scenarios with replicas, his focus is total, and he mentally leaves the room and exists within the context of his knowledge and the action he has created. When we make our pilgrimage to the wall of fossils next summer (he's already planning our trip), I know he will be engrossed and transported by the moment. As for me, I'll be reminded of the boy I was when I saw the Grand Canyon for the first time.

Deep time—the eons of geologic change I hardly understood as a Boy Scout, and the creatures Calvin adores, now only ossified remains—remind me that we're not much more than a blip and that we're visitors here—some with better manners and more morals than others, sure.

But most of us, like me (and my grandson, I'll bet), grow up but never lose our senses of wonder and responsibility. Thank God for national parks. Here's hoping we all do what we can to keep them going.

NOTES

1. "Organic Act of 1916," National Park Service, accessed October 25, 2014, http://www.nps.gov/grba/parkmgmt/organic-act-of-1916.htm

2. Dayton Duncan and Ken Burns, The National Parks: America's Best Idea (New York: Alfred A. Knopf, 2009), 17.

3. "Kilauea Commemorates Twenty-five Years of Volcanic Activity" National Park Service, last modified January 2, 2008, accessed November 11, 2014, http://www.nps.gov/havo/parknews/upload/havo_pr_20080102_anniversary.pdf.

4. Edward Abbey, "Quotations by Author," *A Voice Crying in the Wilderness*, accessed October 25, 2014, http://www.quotationspage.com/quotes/Edward_Abbey/.

5. "Proposition 215," California Department of Public Health, accessed October 25, 2014, http://www.cdph.ca.gov/programs/mmp/pages/compassionateuseact.aspx.

6. Tom Clynes, "Arizona Park 'Most Dangerous' in U.S.," National Geographic, last modified January 13, 2003, accessed October 25, 2014, http://news.nationalgeographic.com/news/2003/01/0110_030113_organpipeclynes.html.

7. Zachary Coile, "National parks' pot farms blamed on cartels/Mexican drug lords find it easier to grow in state than import," *Chronicle Washington Bureau*, last modified November 18, 2005, accessed November 10, 2014, http://www.sfgate.com/news/article/National-parks-pot-farms-blamed-on-cartels-2560508.php.

8. Damon Tabor, "Weed Whackers," *Outside Magazine*, last modified June 2012, accessed November 10, 2014, http://www.outsideonline.com/outdoor-adventure/politics/Weed-Whackers-.html.

9. [Boy Scout], "How to Grow in Forests and Parks," *Marijuana Magazine*, last modified April 12, 2006, accessed November 10, 2014, http://www.cannabisculture.com/articles/4717.html.

7 Cops and Little Robbers

Cop #1—Larry

Larry sat behind the wheel of an aging Chevy Blazer. The lettering on its side, *COUNTY SHERIFF*, was faded from long hours in the desert sun. It was another in a long line of endless days, the officer manning his post for the benefit of the citizens of Orderville, Utah. That's the name of the place, no joke. The Mormons who originally settled there in 1875 followed the United Order program, a strict communal way of life that called for sacrifice, discipline, and well . . . order.

So you could say this cop would have fit right in back then. His was not a glamorous assignment, but speed traps were necessary to get tourists and truckers to slow down as they passed through the sleepy town.

Not that he minded. He didn't have a thought in his head as he stared straight ahead, as unblinking and stoic as Clint Eastwood in a Spaghetti Western. The action unfolded around him in a daily ritual of predictable reactions to his presence. Drivers coming from the north rounded the curve behind him, saw the light bar on the top of his SUV, braked hard and slowed to the required thirty-five miles per hour. Those coming from the south spotted him on the long straightaway and did the same thing.

But one time, something different happened. A silver Toyota RAV4 passed at a crawl, pulled into the parking lane, and backed up a little. A judge from Cedar City got out, tentatively approaching, trying to see through the reflection on the windshield. Pausing a few feet from the SUV, the judge laughed, shook his head, and walked back to his car mumbling, "Busted by a blow-up doll!"

It was just another day at the office for Latex Larry, or so the locals called him.

Cop #2—Where's Waldo?

That same day, a flesh-and-blood cop—lets call him Waldo—sat comfortably in his vehicle: a brand-spanking new Ford F-250, the forest service's standard-issue vehicle for its officers. Waldo was parked some forty miles or so from where Larry was, but rather than sitting on a busy highway in the middle of town, Waldo was eating lunch in the shade cast by nearby towering Ponderosa pines in the middle of Dixie National Forest. The window was down, and he was stretching out his break like he always did. His goal each day was not to stop ATV users from tearing up meadows or arrest people who cut down trees without permits or search for clues to the marijuana grows that were popping up in his jurisdiction. Nope, Waldo didn't give a rip about stopping crime at *any* level. His sole goal each day was to punch in and punch out and thus move one step closer to retirement.

The differences between Larry and Waldo were significant.

Larry could always be found. His Blazer would be at either end of town, usually parked at a slight angle in a conspicuous spot, so the drivers who overlooked the light bar on the roof could see what was spelled out on the passenger doors. He and Latex Lucille, who joined the force a year after Larry, never sat in cafés eating donuts and drinking coffee on the taxpayer's dime. That would have been nice, being with someone like you—flexible, serene, attractive—looking into each other's eyes while playing an endless game of who blinks first, but no—all they got was the bare necessity: air from time to time to fill out those uniforms.

In contrast, Waldo just appeared for work and left at the end of his shift; no one knew what happened in between. He was a more like a mirage that way: something there, but with no substance.

But aside from Larry being made of rubber and Waldo being flesh and blood, the most important difference was that Larry was a hell of a lot better cop than Waldo. Larry actually got speeders to slow down—even local wisenheimers like this judge. Waldo did . . . well, no one is really sure what duties Waldo performed. In the five years he was employed (it would be wrong to say, "In the five years he worked") in my jurisdiction, I couldn't remember him ever writing a ticket. That's right—not one. Waldo lived in the same city, and after a while, it dawned on me that I never saw tickets from him. After a few years on the job, I got curious about it.

"Why don't I ever see violations written up by Waldo in my court? Did I offend him?" The forest service guys were evasive. "Uh, dunno," they'd say. I could never tell if the officers were uncomfortable because they just didn't know, or because they didn't want to diss a comrade. Either way, their time for chitchat was limited; unlike Waldo, they actually *had* cases to discuss.

"Does Waldo even exist?" I would ask.

"Oh yes," Roger would say. "He's actually a nice guy."

"What does he do for eight hours a day?"

Roger hadn't a clue.

Perhaps the most important difference between Waldo and Larry is best explained by modern civic economy. Enforcement personnel often take the hit for faulty budget management, and so jobs are given to earnest—but let's face it—inert plastic people. In other words, Larry didn't cost the taxpayers any money. He just sat in the nice sheriff's car, warmed by the sunshine, inflating as the heat built in the squad car and deflating as the sun set. Waldo drew a salary with benefits, drove around in a gas-guzzling SUV, and contributed to the national deficit with nothing to show for it. He is now retired, although the end result is pretty much the same as far as crimes detected, arrests made, and convictions entered.

But of course there are some similarities between Larry and Waldo too, the most significant ones being that they both spent a career just sitting on their butt and—let's be honest here—neither one had a conscience.

Cop #3—You "Otto" Get a Conscience

I know something about having a conscience.

Saturday matinees were a tradition in Cedar City in the 1950s and '60s. If you were a grade-school kid with fifteen cents in your pocket, you spent Saturday afternoon at the Cedar Theater with other kids from all three elementary schools. Kids went to the matinees because you got to see a cool cartoon, a lame serial like Flash Gordon that no one watched, but which gave you time to get to the mezzanine balcony and throw Boston Baked Beans or Dots down at your friends—or, even better—at the cute girls from different schools. Then you settled in with your friends for the featured movie—usually a Western—that had been made sometime in the last five years.

The Cedar Theater was a cavernous throwback to a gilded age, with a stage and curtains that had to be physically drawn back before the projectors were turned on. Occasionally, an especially rambunctious kid would run up to the stage mid-movie and do a tap-dance or shadow-animal rendition in front of the screen, and half of the audience would cheer and the half who were actually watching the movie would boo, until finally the owner—overweight, balding, and looking to be in mid-cardiac arrest—would throw the kid out the side exit.

It was located smack-dab in the commercial epicenter of Cedar City—*all* of Iron County for that matter. Starting at Center and Main and moving north, you had JCPenney, where pretty much everything you were wearing had been bought by your mother. Next door was Woolworth's Five & Dime, where you cruised for toys and candy while your mom bought stuff that wasn't provided by either Leigh Furniture or Lin's Grocery just down the block. Then there was the Kandy Kitchen with sodas and shakes that only high schoolers could afford, and next door to that was the Cedar Theater.

Bobby and Clyde lived four blocks from this commercial hub. They were best friends. They were also the two who had come up with the sell-two-cent-candy-bars-for-a-nickel scheme back on Dewey Avenue. One Saturday, while walking to a matinee, they whined to each other about the unfair price of movie candy. What were they to do? Setting up a card table in the theater to sell their own candy wasn't an option, but *something* had to give, they agreed. They chewed it over. Woolworth's was right there on the way to the movie, and *their* prices were fair, so why not buy something at Woolworth's and sneak it in? Then one of them (and it doesn't matter which one, they were in this together as best buds) said why not *steal* some candy for the movie? By the time they got to Woolworth's they had a scheme which scared and thrilled them at the same time—they'd never done anything like it before.

They knew the clerk would be as suspicious as a mother if they just handled some stuff at the candy aisle and then left the store without buying anything. So, as planned, they picked up a Charms in one hand, palmed a Life Savers roll in the other (it fit so naturally inside the curved fingers!) walked toward the clerk saying, "I want to buy this," while simultaneously holding up the Charms for her to look at and sticking their other hand in a pocket, pulling out a nickel, and leaving the Life Savers roll in its place.

It worked—slick as a whistle! Even though they felt guilty, another part of them felt tough and clever, and so they did it again the next week.

And then Otto Fife paid a visit.

In the middle of the next school week, all of the third- and fourth-graders at West Elementary were herded into the multi-purpose room and told to sit on the rug. Otto Fife, the Iron County Sheriff, was making the rounds and talking at all the schools.

He was a tall, kind man with a penchant for telling corny but interesting stories, and he was in full uniform. Probably. All that the kids could remember afterward was his face and the big gun on his hip. He regaled them with tales of crimes foiled and bandits caught by the Iron County Sheriff and his deputies. The kids loved every story. It was better than the matinees! But, at the end of his talk, he turned serious and started pacing the front of the room, head turned and looking at us one at a time.

"We know what goes on in this town. We know who breaks the law, and I need to warn you: every murderer started by committing small crimes." He had our attention. Nobody was poking anyone else or talking.

"You start with something small, and then you do something bigger, and if you get away with it, you just keep going and going until you end up in prison! And trust me, you don't want to go there!"

Bobby about peed his pants, expecting to be handcuffed at any second.

At recess, Bobby ran up to Clyde. "He knows what we did!"

"I know!"

"We can't do it again."

"We have to repent and pray!" said Clyde, the more religious of the two (not a close contest).

"Okay . . . ," Bobby said.

And then one of them had another idea: "Let's give the money back!"

And so they did. It ended up being as easy as stealing the candy in the first place. They went to Woolworth's, bought a five-cent roll of Life Savers (they had found that Charms actually sucked—they were just square lifesavers individually wrapped but without any flavor), paid with a nickel, and, while the clerk was busy ringing up the sale, each put a dime to the side of the cash register where the cashier couldn't miss it later. Both were relieved to have escaped prison and to get back to just being a kid.

One became an attorney and a judge. The other went on to be an attorney and a CPA and then budget director to the governor of the state of Utah. Later, he was appointed to be the first director of Utah's College Savings Plan, overseeing hundreds of millions of dollars. Bobby and Clyde never pulled another caper.

Or so I thought, until forty-plus years later when I read in the *Salt Lake Tribune* that Clyde had pled guilty to pilfering $85,000 out of the College Savings Plan into his own account and was headed for jail. I was dumbfounded. Clyde was a bright person and a gifted athlete. His wife was a sweetheart (the three of us were all in the same third-grade class together), he came from a great family—*and* he repaid the state's money. He just should have listened to Otto.

And who knows, maybe meeting a dedicated cop like Otto early on in life could have saved other kids who later ended up standing before a judge in court as adults.

Cop #4—How to Ruin a Great Party

It was past midnight, and everybody had a good buzz going. There was a little cocaine, a few joints, and lots and lots of beer. In other words— it was a typical southern Utah blowout. Pickups were parked every which way in a wide circle around a bonfire. This spot was chosen because it was in a depression in a pinon and juniper forest. To get there, you had to drive on a jeep track and then go off the road a ways (all the better to avoid detection). Only two of the thirteen boys were over twenty-one, and they didn't want to get busted again.

A few brought .22 rifles and had target practice, shooting at empty Coors and Budweiser cans lit up by headlights. Others just chilled or visited or listened to the country-Western music coming from an open pickup door.

A good time was had by all until Mark Harris, a BLM ranger, walked into the light, armed, in uniform, and holding up his badge. "This party is over. I need to see everybody's identification," he said.

Well, you'd have thought Paul Bunyan had just pissed out the bonfire the way everybody grumbled, threw away joints, and side-stepped away from open cans of beer as if to say, "I don't know what *that's* doing here!" But they complied. He wrote them all tickets, they signed for them, and he let those who'd barely registered on the portable breath tests drive those who were worse off home rather than try to haul everybody to jail.

As the boys left, one of them asked, "How did you find us? We hid pretty good."

"Shrewd detective work," he said, tapping a finger on the side of his skull. "Plus the fact you had a bonfire, pickup lights, loud music, gun-shots that were reported, and you ended up only two miles from Highway 18 as the crow flies."

"Oh!" they said.

When they came to court, most pled guilty; two marijuana-smokers pled not guilty and were surprised at trial to find that Harris could correctly draw a diagram of where they were sitting. He told how he'd watched them smoke during the time he had done a quick reconnaissance around the gathering, determined how many people were there, and how best to make his approach.

After court, I asked Harris to come back to his chambers.

"You're getting a reputation," I said.

"I am?"

"Yup. The other day, my son asked me if I knew some super cop that works around here."

Harris grinned and raised an eyebrow.

"He said a couple of his friends were at a kegger at Baker's Reservoir. They thought they were safe because they were being quiet, when all of a sudden this BLM cop pops up out of nowhere and busts them for being minors with alcohol. They said he was a weird skinny dude, about five-ten, and maybe 150 pounds, bald-headed and wearing night goggles. At first they were scared of him because he looked so strange, and they were caught red-handed, but then after he left, they were like, 'wait a minute, there was one of him and, like, fifteen of us—*he* should have been scared.'"

"Weird skinny dude?"

"I thought you'd like that."

"Super cop?"

"His words, not mine."

Harris smiled and got up to leave.

"I hear you're transferring to California."

"Have to. It's a promotion, and I could use the money. But I loved it here. Better than Louisiana, Texas, or Arizona."

"Be careful. I worry about you going out alone at night. What if things go bad?"

"I know what I'm doing."

And he does. He's tough as nails and wrote more tickets—and they were solid—than anybody I had run across. Not all midnight busts are of relatively nice kids sowing their wild oats like the judge's son's friends. Harris knows this. He's busted far worse.

Let's hope his luck doesn't take a turn for the worse, like Kris Eggle, the ranger at Organ Pipe Cactus National Park who was cut down by drug dealers in 2003. Just this past spring I spoke to a group of rangers from various national parks, including Organ Pipe, and was reminded of him. Eggle now has a visitor center named after him. Appropriate, but tragic.

Common opinion has it that cops eventually become jaded—or worn down to where they don't do much more than Waldo. I think that's an overgeneralization, and Otto and Harris flew in the face of that. Otto is long deceased now. I was lucky to have known him as a kid, an attorney, and as a hiking companion. And here's hoping that Harris is still walking a beat or popping up in the middle of a drug party in his night goggles. The world needs more cops like him.

8 You Be the Jury

You go to the mailbox to see what has washed up in today's bulk-rate tide, reach in, and start sifting as you amble back to the house: clothing catalogs, unsolicited credit card offers, donation requests from fringe charity groups with nickels glued to them. Then you see it—and hear that sound in your head like a submarine diving to avoid a torpedo, *Ah-oogah! Ah-oogah!*—a summons for jury duty with your name on it.

Well, it's good that I'm here to help. We'll have a little sidebar conference, you and I, in this chapter. So read on. Remember, you can trust me. I'm a lawyer.

1. Enjoy the doughnuts.

A few years back at a judicial conference, I attended a breakout group entitled, "Keeping Jurors Happy." Our state had recently adopted a system of surveying jurors, post-verdict, to find out what they thought of their trial judge. The state then published the results just before our names were put on the ballot for a retention vote. Hence, my heightened interest in the happiness of my jurors. The lecturer was a seasoned judge from New Jersey, with ample jowls, a deep, raspy baritone voice, and long silver hair, combed straight back to curl around his collar. He reminded me somewhat of Sam Ervin of the Watergate hearings, except without the southern drawl. "If you don't remember anything else from my lecture," he began, "remember this: *always* buy doughnuts.

"Have your bailiff or clerk pick up the doughnuts," he continued. "Pay them back out of your own pocket if the court won't reimburse you." And then he moved on to more intellectual aspects of pleasing jurors, none of which I remember. I took him at his word and just remembered his first bit of advice, and it's been gold.

Pull people off their jobs, subject them to personal examination by attorneys (*What magazines do you buy? What TV shows do you watch? Are you married? Divorced? How many times?*), tell them they belong to you for the next so many days, and then put them in a small room with nothing but tepid tap water and Dixie cups, and you've got understandable resentment brewing.

Have the same nervous juror enter the jury room mid-morning to find an open cardboard box filled with éclairs, alligator jaws, maple bars, or chocolate-covered donuts doused with rainbow colored sprinkles or sliced almonds—yum! You've got an entirely different atmosphere. I'm not being condescending here. Being a quick learner, I found that if I picked up a large box of doughnuts for the jury with a bag on the side for me, the bailiff, and the clerk, we were happier too. To hell with nutrition! Justice is fueled by comfort food.

2. Stick up for yourself.

No one knows your situation better than you. Sometimes the judge might innocently act against your own best interest, so stand up for yourself as long as it's within the rules of the court.

For instance, I was screening potential jurors once for a two-week trial and had just begun putting final questions to a specific juror: a frail, frightened, teenage girl whose written jury questionnaire said she was a single mother working at a local drive-in.

I felt she deserved a little help, so I told her, "We've ended up with more jurors than we need. I'm wondering if I should excuse you." I looked at the attorneys to see if they objected. They didn't and nodded their approval. My intention was to allow her to earn her paycheck to provide for her and her baby. After all, like most states, Utah paid a pittance to jurors—$18.50 for the first day and $49.00 every day thereafter. (And no, I don't know what's with the fifty cents.)

Her face fell. "Please don't! I'll make more here than at the *Dairy Freeze*."

I was glad she spoke up and was also glad to find that I wasn't the only one moved by her comments. After the attorneys had used their peremptory challenges (excusing a juror without stating a reason—each side gets a few) she remained on the jury.

3. You are neither more nor less important than the other potential jurors.

Every once in a while, I run across a juror who is a complete jerk. Understandable, since the only selection criteria for the jury pool is a random cross-section from voter registration lists and drivers license rolls. We all know jerks vote and change lanes to cut you off on the freeway.

The least cooperative juror I can remember sat in my courtroom making noises (grunt, scoff, then look at the ceiling) while he was waiting to be called. I should have straightened him out then, but I was concentrating on the group I was filtering from the gallery up into the jury box. When his name was called, he sashayed on up like he was a movie star surrounded by extras. His cocky strut and demeanor were at odds with his physical appearance: homely, extremely pale complexion, bald on top with long, recently permed blond hair—kind of like a bowl of old spaghetti had been dumped on his head.

"I don't have time for this," he announced before I could ask any preliminary questions. "I own a motel, and time is money."

"Okay," I said, "but let me ask you a few questions."

Agitated, he shifted his weight from one foot to the other and glowered at me in frustration. "I guess you don't understand. I own a motel. I supervise the maids and the clerks. Without me, things can go wrong, and I lose money."

"Everybody here has a job," I said, motioning to the jurors who had already been questioned and were sitting in the jury box. "No one juror is more important than another based on how much they are paid."

The other jurors nodded their approval, which is when I think he remembered he'd be sequestered with his new enemies and changed tactics: "I can't be fair. I don't want to be here, so I'll hold it against him," he said, pointing at the defendant, who was clearly entitled at that point to have him removed.

I was infuriated. I was outmaneuvered from a legal standpoint—but not from a coach's standpoint. I benched him. "Fine," I said. "You are excused from jury duty because of your bias against the defendant. But you're not leaving this courtroom. Take a seat on the back row. If you try to leave this courtroom without permission, I'll have you arrested for contempt of court. You're going to listen to this trial all the way through, just like these jurors. At the end of the trial, you'll have an opinion of what the verdict should be just like them. The only difference is that your opinion won't matter."

The bailiff stepped forward and escorted him to a bench seat under a clock on the wall. When I'd check the time every once in a while, I could see him as well. He went from stunned and angry to compliant, listening to the testimony despite himself.

I've only had to use that choleric posture one other time, but the attitude of the second juror was much different at the end. A stay-at-home-mom—with a babysitter for the day—demanded she be allowed to leave and started to make a scene. As with the motel owner, I made her stay. But as she watched the trial, her physical posture softened, and she began leaning forward to take in the testimony. I couldn't help but notice, and at the lunch break I asked her if she had any thoughts. She said she had acted out and was sorry. She also said the trial was fascinating, and she wished she was on the jury. I told her she was free to go and that I appreciated her understanding how important jury trials were. She was a good citizen; she'd just had a poor mind-set.

4. Read the fine print.

Jury instructions are like the owner's manual in your new car. You may not want to sit down and read the manual from cover to cover, but it will inevitably come in handy when you need to change the oil or determine *which* secret compartment contains the tire jack, and you need to know *now*.

The judge uses jury instructions to explain the law you will apply to the case. You'll get a copy when you deliberate at the end. At times you'll wish you hadn't. They are detailed and very necessary and boring as . . . well, an owner's manual. If I make the mistake of making eye contact with the jury after reading the lengthy final instructions, I will see expressions that range from catatonic stares to homicidal rage, depending on the attention span of the individual juror involved. But they work, and no one has come up with anything better. So follow them. You'll be a better juror if you do. In the next section we'll see what happens when you don't.

And remember: I apologize. Really, I do.

5. Don't hijack the trial!

It's important that you follow the jury instructions. A key instruction will say something like this: "Your decision must be made from the evidence, or lack thereof, produced here in court." Ignore this concept and you can convict the innocent or free the guilty, which is only fine if it's the premise for a movie.

Take, for example, The Case of the Visiting Professor. He ended up on one of my juries, and he totally derailed the case, which was especially bothersome because he was a friend of mine. Originally from Ireland, he'd married a Cedar City girl whom he'd met in graduate school. Our families were friends.

It was a drunk-driving trial with a slam dunk set of facts for the prosecution: a bad driving pattern, multiple failed field sobriety tests, and a breathalyzer test reading *way* beyond the margin of error for the machine.

At the end of the trial, the jury began deliberations, and I retired to chambers, where I waited and waited long after catching up on my paperwork. Eventually I wandered back into the courtroom, no robe and tie loosened, and plopped down in my seat. The attorneys were shooting the breeze at counsel table while their sidekicks for the day, the arresting officer and the defendant, gazed off in opposite directions and then slowly directed their attention at me with numbed expressions. Apparently listening to attorneys talk shop isn't all that riveting.

"Any idea why this is taking so long?" I asked.

The prosecutor fidgeted, and the defense attorney smiled.

"No—but I'm liking it."

"Did I miss something?" I asked. "I thought the prosecution had this one locked down."

"So did I," said the prosecutor.

"Me too," the defense attorney confessed. "But you never know with a jury—that's why I asked for one." The defendant shot an angry look at his attorney, but he shouldn't have. His attorney had done a good job and was just being honest. Understand that if the prosecution has only a twenty percent chance of winning a case, they have no business filing it. But the reverse is true for a defense attorney, where twenty percent odds are good for a defendant. (National average for convictions in federal criminal jury trials? Estimates vary, but it's generally agreed to be ninety-plus percent.)

Later that night, the jury finally delivered its startling verdict: not guilty.

A few weeks later, I had the chance to ask the English professor's daughter if her father had said anything to her about the case. She was a bright, spunky girl and was not the least bit intimidated by my being a judge. In fact, my daughters' friends usually called me "Judge Bob" with a little bit of affection. Or so I'd like to think.

"Did he explain how they found the defendant *not* guilty despite the overwhelming evidence?"

She rolled her eyes. "He said the prosecution didn't prove its case! He told the jury that he'd heard of a study once that said alcohol could get caught in a space in the mouth—like a hole in a tooth or filling—and then get released hours later when the person blew into the machine."

Dumbfounded, I said, "First of all, I don't believe any such study exists, and second, even if it did, the jury shouldn't have considered it because it wasn't entered into evidence! The prosecution didn't get a chance to rebut that argument."

Nonplussed, she went on. "Plus, he doesn't believe in field sobriety tests."

"No?"

"No! When he was in graduate school he earned extra money by volunteering to be in some alcohol demonstrations for cops or something."

"Let me guess—he told the jury about this too."

"Of course."

"Was it an alcohol impairment demonstration where they give the first guy one drink, and the second guy two drinks, and so on, and then they have them perform field sobriety tests?"

"Yeah, something like that! And they gave him a bunch of drinks to mess him up, but he passed all of the tests and confused the instructors!"

Alarmed, and worried about her father, I said, "Katelyn—that's the definition of a 'functional alcoholic!'"

"No, Judge Bob," she fired back immediately. "That's the definition of an Irishman."

Individual jurors can sometimes make or break the case in ways attorneys and judges have no way of anticipating. When I was an attorney, my wife got empanelled on an attempted murder case. I was surprised, since the attorneys in the case were friends of ours, but I guess they both thought she'd do fine. It was a two-day trial, which ended in a deadlocked jury and a mistrial. I scrupulously followed the mandate of not trying to influence jurors and said nothing to her about the case until it was over. The next day, I repeated a question the prosecutor had asked me when he collared me in the courthouse. "Jim asked me how it was that the jury was deadlocked."

"Before we even sat down in the jury room, two men on the jury announced that they would never vote 'guilty.'"

"But he says the defendant confessed that he 'pointed the gun at center mass and pulled the trigger!'"

"That's true, but those jurors said the defendant was drunk, and that they've been drunk, and you don't know what you're doing when you're drunk."

"But I'm sure you had a 'Voluntary Intoxication' instruction that said drinking doesn't let a person off the hook."

"Yeah, but they said Utah has screwed up liquor laws and people here don't know what it's like in the real world. They wouldn't budge."

It's startling, really, how often drinkers are ready and willing to set people straight about alcohol—particularly in Utah.

And it's not a *Utah* rule—or instruction—it's a universal rule. Substitute your own rule, and you're not in the state of Utah, you're in a state of chaos. Follow the instructions, and you'll be giving society a better chance that justice will be done.

6. Focus During Deliberations.

After you've heard the evidence and retire with the other jurors to reach a just verdict, focus. I know this seems like a lot to ask. You've been ordered to and fro, been told where to sit, when to eat, heck—even when you can pee. You finally have your intellectual freedom, a chance to speak frankly, and you want to have your say. Fine. That's what we *want* you to do. But stay focused.

I've had juries in felony trials send written notes to me via the bailiff while they were in the midst of deliberations: (1) wondering when they would be fed (this at 4:30 p.m.!), and (2) asking why they were provided Cokes, but no Pepsis. The worst, though, was when a jury had deliberated for hours, and the attorneys and I couldn't figure out why. It was a simple debt collection case: either you believed the retailer or you didn't. Finally, I told my clerk to go into the jury room and ask if they were nearing a verdict. "Don't tell us anything they're saying, just get in and get out."

She returned, announcing to the whole courtroom, "They're arguing about whether it's faster to send Christmas packages by UPS or Fed Ex."

"What!"

"I think they were embarrassed. They said they were almost done."

You'll do everyone a favor by sticking to the subject.

7. Know it can get ugly—and try not to personalize it.

Jurors have to sit through all kinds of cases, some featuring attorneys wrangling over legal minutiae, some concerning gut-wrenching, horrific crimes and exhibits *no one* wants to look at, but someone has to. I once halted a jury trial in a capital homicide because the bailiff handed me a note that said, "Juror needs to throw up. Recess." I recessed, and she promptly recessed to the ladies room across the hall from my chambers. I'm sure all of the other jurors, like me, were secretly thankful for a chance to regain their composure.

The juror? That Dairy Freeze waitress who had begged to be on the jury to earn a few extra dollars for her and her baby. The criminal trial had become a personal trial for her as well.

A day in court can range from humorous to tedious to heartbreaking. In the end, we are all human beings dealing with other human beings, too often learning about the worst that humans can do to each other.

But think of this: the most frequent comment I have heard from jurors over the years is: "I didn't want to serve, but now that I have, I'm really glad I did." And I'm glad they did. A bond develops between the judge and the jurors, and I watch them with empathy as they take the ultimate trial burden from my shoulders. It's an unfamiliar sensation—the weight of a legal decision—but you'll be able to share it with your peers, and the judge will try to move the stones out of your path so you don't stumble. You'll get through it together.

9 On Judging

Stephen Colbert: "You're a Supreme Court Justice. I'm not. That gives you the right to judge things."

Justice John Paul Stevens: "That's right."

Stephen Colbert: "That's very convenient."

Justice John Paul Stevens: "That's part of your commission—you have to do some judging."

—Colbert Report, January 19, 2012[1]

One night in 2009, my wife and I were watching a special news report about the newly elected president on NBC—*Inside the Obama White House*—when I received a phone call.

"This is Special Agent Lemon with the Secret Service," an unfamiliar voice said. "I have a complaint and warrant of arrest I'd like to bring to you. I'm in St. George and I can be there in an hour." The Secret Service making a house call at my house? This was a first.

I logged onto the computer, anxious to see the paperwork he'd emailed to me, spelling out the crime charged: "Threats against the President of the United States." I had an immediate, visceral response. Like a lot of Americans, I vividly remember the Kennedy assassination and the attempt on Reagan.

The defendant had opened a savings account with an $85,000 cashier's check while warning the teller, "With all this mess going on under President Obama with banks and the economy, I'm sure if citizens happen to lose their money, they will rise up and we could see killing and deaths." He withdrew all the cash the following week, demanding the bills be no larger than fifty dollars "in non-sequential order." Cash in hand, he said, "We are on a mission to kill the President of the United States." He was known to carry several forms of identification and had at least eight firearms registered to him, "all easy to conceal," according to the affidavit. The president was scheduled to speak at a fundraiser for Senator Harry Reid in Las Vegas—a two-hour drive from St. George—two days later.

I'd arranged some seating on the front lawn by the time the agent arrived, the better to enjoy a cool summer evening with the sun setting behind us, and I read through the documents he'd brought. Everything seemed in order. He was an earnest and competent young guy, I could tell, even without the black suit and wrist walkie-talkie.

"Raise your right hand," I said, preparing to have him take an oath as to what was stated in the affidavit and complaint. "Do you swear that the allegations contained in these documents are true and correct to the best of your knowledge and belief?"

"I do."

I wondered momentarily what the neighbors might think, seeing two guys in khakis and polo shirts, squared off in lawn chairs doing the truth-and-whole-truth salute.

"Do you have a fax machine?" he asked when we'd affixed our signatures to the complaint. "Washington wanted a copy of this as soon as it was signed."

Unfortunately my fax and scanner were both down. I offered to have my son-in-law open up his pharmacy office, but the agent remembered a Marriott hotel near the freeway.

"I'm sure they'll let me use their fax machine."

I had no doubt about that. The night clerk would be telling this story in the break room for the next month.

So we shook hands and off he went.

Before going to bed, I made one last check of my emails. I found a report from a ranger at Lake Powell regarding the arrest of a teenager from Page, Arizona, who had decided to throw rocks at ducks at Lone Rock Beach. He hit one in the head, injuring it badly. Then he'd run. The duck was flopping around in pain and making awful noises that upset a nearby picnicking couple, who tried to put the duck out of its misery. However, dispatching the duck proved tougher to accomplish and was noisier than expected.

Many nearby picnickers didn't witness the original attack, so they deluged 911 with reports about a red-faced man wringing an innocent bird's neck, and officers converged on the scene. After sorting things out, they tracked the kid down and confronted him about the duck stoning. Why? They'd asked. He'd shrugged and said, "I don't know." It was the kind of day that gets you thinking about the range of lunacy and motivation (or lack of it) that Pandora let loose in the world when she opened that box.

Oh, and what happened to the duck stoner and would-be assassin? The duck stoner ended up being a minor, so the case was transferred to juvenile court where he was fined. The man who threatened the president had a history of serious mental illness, and I ordered him to undergo a mental health assessment with the Board of Prisons. After a lengthy and difficult period of treatment and medication adjustments, he stabilized. By agreement of both sides he was released to his parents, who had driven from upstate New York to be in attendance in the courtroom. These were the same people who had a restraining order against their son for prior violent acts. They had lived in constant fear of him before his arrest and treatment. Seeing that he was receiving treatment and was going to be cared for by people who loved him made for a feel-good day for everyone in the courtroom.

Some people have wondered why I'd give up my job as a state trial judge, in which I had much more authority, and a lot more pressure, to become a US magistrate. Some of the judges I worked with in the state system wondered if, in fact, I had lost my mind when I made the change. Judge for yourself. The following exhibits from my time as a state trial judge, illustrate why I chose to shift careers:

Exhibit A: A burly man with unruly hair and borderline intelligence follows me up and down the aisle of the grocery store, muttering quietly until I turn to him and say, "What can I do for you Mr. Spainhower?"

He looks startled to find me aware of his surveillance and of his identity even though he was often in my court on both felonies and misdemeanors. "I don't think I should have to pay that fine," he says.

I invite him to come to court on Monday to talk it over, where I'll have an armed bailiff present who has my back when I deliver the bad news that the fine is still owed.

Years later, I'm checking my mailbox after lunch and notice a car parked across the street. My vision isn't the best anymore, and I can't quite ID the guy at the wheel, but the car follows me back to work, and just like in the movies I take down the license plate number on the back of an envelope as I drive.

Bailiff Charley Young, runs the number for me. "Geez, Judge, that guy is 10-46!"

"What the hell does 10-46 mean?"

"He's crazy. It's Gary Spainhower, and he just got out of prison."

Frightening, yes. I have a family, after all. Grown and gone now, but for all those years, their safety and well-being weighed in the back of my mind.

Exhibit B: Being on the bench adjudicating the break-up of families took a toll, too. Take the all-too-frequent case of two flawed but decent parents who can't get along and just one of them should get custody: a deal where they both agree that's what has to happen, they just disagree on *who* it should be. I'd make my decision, feeling confident I did the right thing, but then a year later I'm in that same grocery store, bagging golden delicious apples, when I feel someone staring at me. I look up with an apple in my hand and lock eyes briefly with a man across the way. For a second the face doesn't register, and then I remember that's the father I *didn't* award custody to, and this is obviously his weekend for visitation because there he is with two cute little kids riding in the grocery cart he's pushing, and before he looks away, I see pain in his eyes that is palpable.

The worst of the divorce cases involved claims of sexual child-abuse by the father. Cases with evidence heavily weighted one way or the other seldom went to trial, they were settled out of court. Only those that could go either way end up being litigated in my courtroom. There weren't many, but, oh, how I hated them. I did my best, but I was haunted by the thought that some twenty years later the now-adult child of that divorce would come up to me and say, "Judge Braithwaite, you made a mistake. I never really got to know my father growing up because of you—*and he never touched me!*" Or worse yet, "You left me in a house to be molested by my father over and over again." It hasn't happened yet. I hope it never does.

Exhibit C: I honestly thought I'd never have to decide whether a defendant lived or died when I served as a state judge. *Judges* just try the case, but *juries* decide whether to use the death penalty. Or so I thought, until, during one capital homicide case, a prosecutor and defense counsel jointly moved to waive the jury for the sentencing phase of a capital homicide case.

I immediately convened a sidebar conference. "No!" I told them, settling the matter. "That issue has to be decided by a jury."

"With all due respect, Your Honor . . . ," they said, and then proceeded to explain that under a new Utah law, if both sides in a death penalty case agreed to waive the jury, the judge had to make the decision. "I don't want to make that decision," I told them. They nodded in agreement and said they didn't blame me, but that my hands were tied. I looked at the statute and had to agree. I don't think I said it out loud, but I remember thinking at the time, "One of you is making a mistake. You (the defense attorney) are hoping I don't have the guts to impose the death penalty, and you (the prosecutor) are hoping I don't have the compassion for the defendant *not* to." I felt sick to my stomach as they walked back to their counsel tables.

I'll go to my grave thinking I made the right decision, but also wishing I hadn't had to make it. If an appellate court wants to take that decision off my shoulders, I'll have no complaint. But they haven't so far. It's been thirteen years.

I could have retired from the bench rather than opt for the part-time work as a magistrate. Easier said than done. I remember Dan Becker, the court administrator for Utah, telling me he never believed a judge when that judge said he was going to retire. When he saw the shock on my face, he explained. "It's not that I think they are lying to me—I respect judges. All I can tell you is that saying you are going to give up being a judge and actually doing it are two different things. I believe they are retiring when I get the written notification." He smiled wryly.

So why the reluctance to retire?

I would be guilty of omission if I didn't confess certain perks that go along with judgeships. Say you're tired of hearing people yammer on and on. You can say, "I've heard enough argument; I am ready to rule," and they stop talking. And these people are *attorneys!* And then, too, the ego stroking isn't exactly painful: people call you "Your Honor," they stand when you enter the room, and *they laugh at your jokes.*

As one spoilsport lecturer at my new-judge boot camp at the National Judicial College put it: "You think everyone laughs at your jokes now because you've suddenly become funnier?"

Also, for some of us, part of the reluctance to retire has to do with the very reasons we gave when we applied for the job. We wanted challenging, interesting, and important work. Call us idealistic if you must, but we really did want *to make a difference.*

And let's face it, all of us get attached to who and what we've become. I remember reading a front-page article in the *Salt Lake Tribune* about the Chief Justice of the Utah Supreme Court and his decision to leave the bench and pursue other interests, like mediation. He made a comment to the effect that, "I couldn't sleep one night as retirement was approaching, and didn't know exactly why. Then it hit me, and I told my wife the answer: 'The judge is dying.'"

What a crock, I thought. *How egotistical—I'll never think like that. Judge is just a job description.* Well, wrong again, I found out. I've gotten used to folks bumping into me, saying, "Hey, judge, how you doin'? So judges have to eat lunch too, huh?" You quit, and, well, you're gone. As another lecturer at that same judicial boot camp put it: "Your robes are rented. People don't call you 'Your Honor' and rise because you are inherently wonderful—it's the *position* that is honored."

The morning of my first divorce case I left my home reluctantly. I told my wife, "I'm going to ruin a decent person's life today."

"What do you mean?" she asked. "You don't *have* to ruin someone's life, surely."

"It's a divorce case. I've read the home studies prepared by a social worker. Both parents are decent but flawed people who love their kids. The parents can't get along at all, both agree joint custody won't work, and they assert that *they* should get custody with visitation given the other parent. Somebody's going to be devastated when I rule."

We held the trial. It was close. Parents and social workers testified. I went back and forth as the evidence came in. Not wanting to continue the trial for half of the next day, we worked into the evening. The final witness was the mother of the wife. She was also an experienced social worker. With a break in her voice, she opined that as much as she loved her daughter, her grandchildren would be better off with her son-in-law.

I deliberated and then awarded custody to the father—not solely because of his mother-in-law's testimony, but it was a key factor.

Then I retired to chambers feeling wrung out. The trial had gone so long that my wife had come and sat in the audience for the last hour. She came back to chambers quite distraught and said, "Do you know what happened in the courtroom after you left?"

"Of course not. I don't know what happens in there when I am in chambers."

"The wife collapsed and is still sobbing uncontrollably! It wasn't just theatrics. She was devastated to lose her children!"

"I know. That's why I said this morning I'm going to ruin a decent person's life today. A decision needs to be made, and it's my job"

The task to "convict the guilty, free the innocent, and place kids in the right home" is not always a clear-cut decision, and I assume the weight of that so that attorneys and litigants and juries don't have to.

A functioning, moral society depends on a small cadre of men and women who are willing to shoulder the burden of being the one who must render a decision. That is why the office merits respect.

So I'm happy in my semi-retirement, to be Honorable only half the time—king of the misdemeanors and proud of it. Four distinctly different courthouses and courtrooms, five national parks, BASE jumpers, big game poachers, cases involving the president of the United States, and ducks (the last two all in the same night!)—I mean, what's not to like? Plus, being half-time, it lets me lead my other life in a way that creates a nice balance. There's a 'struction project outside my back door with a foreman that needs a helper, and I'm gonna be that guy as long as Jack will have me. I mean, that's *honorable* too, right?

And on the days when I'm not called to be a foreman, Dinosaur National Monument guide, or on-duty grandpa, I get to fall back on the best job in the judiciary: night court at the national parks.

NOTES

1. John Paul Stevens, "Colbert Super PAC," Colbert Nation video, January 19, 2012, http://thecolbertreport.cc.com/videos/k3pbui/carrie-rebora-barratt.

BONUS MATERIAL: Real-World Descriptions of Legal Terms

The first Latin phrase I ever heard in law school was *Res Judicata* (pronounced Rez-joo-deh-ka-ta). Literally it means, "A thing adjudged," although my professor defined it as "the law of the case." It's a pretty straightforward fundamental premise of law, actually; what's been decided in a case can't be reargued in the same case or in another between the two parties, or the lawyers, judges, and juries would be stuck in court forever. But I was left wondering, "Why not just say 'the law of the case?' Then *everyone* will know what you mean."

This wouldn't be the only occasion I'd wonder about the incomprehensible jargon of my profession and, frankly, feel empathetic toward laypeople forced for one reason or another to deal with our judicial system.

Just about everybody ends up in court at some point, contesting a traffic ticket or suing your ex-best friend to collect the money your new best friend warned you not to loan or serving on a jury, which suddenly makes getting a root canal seem preferable.

I know. I understand. You're confused and intimidated. And annoyed. And you should be: jargon is one way to keep people in their places. Them (lawyers, doctors, insurance agents) vs. You, the person who pays our bills. (Quick lawyer joke: An angry attorney shows up at the pearly gates and demands to know why he is there. Saint Peter says, "Old age."

The man says, "I eat right, exercise regularly, and I'm fifty-five years old!"

St. Peter checks the ledger and says, "Nope, we counted up your billable hours and you're ninety-seven.")

After graduating from law school, I discovered that sometimes laymen unwittingly protect this linguistic system of haves and have-nots.

91

Returning to my hometown at twenty-five, I hung up my shingle and moved into a one-room office. I had no money for a secretary, but I had my IBM Selectric and could type seventy words per minute. I sat at my desk, reading over divorce forms, contract forms, anything I could get my hands on, so that I would appear busy should anyone enter. Not a single person walked into my office the first week. Well—that's not true. I was next to a Sears outlet store in a very small strip mall, and one of their customers got lost, wandered into my office, and asked where the restroom was. Happy for the company, I spoke to him as long as I could.

As I sat at my desk, shuffling papers and getting ready to give a hearty welcome each time I heard a floor creak, it dawned on me that people who regularly needed an attorney in my hometown already had one, and that building a law practice was going to take time. So, the second week I figured, "What the hell," put my feet up on the desk, and read Louis L'Amour and Robert Ludlum paperbacks. But I hedged my bets. I put the books inside a legal file so that if anyone walked in on me, they would think I was reviewing a case file. I felt like a kid reading *Playboy* inside *The Sporting News*.

Finally, Wendell Brooksby, a veterinarian I'd known since I was a little boy, walked in and asked me to draw up a contract for him. I was flattered to do so. I'd been his paperboy, and he'd cared for my pet beagle over the years, and now he wanted me to be his attorney. I *was* making progress. The contract I drafted was three-and-a-half pages long, and I wrote up a bill for forty-five dollars. I figured he'd turn me in to the cops for charging so much, but I needed money.

When he came back, he read through the document with a growing look of disapproval.

Deflated, I asked, "What's the matter?"

"This contract says what I wanted, but why did you put *Buyer* and *Seller*?"

"I don't think I'm following you," I said, confused.

"Whenever Pat Fenton (picture Raymond Burr, but at twice the volume) used to do a contract for me, it said, *Party of the First Part* and *Party of the Second Part*."

"I'm just trying to keep things simpler and more straightforward," I said. "This way, you don't have to do a mental two-step and think, 'Let's see now, who's the Party of the First Part? Oh yeah, that's me. I'm the party that's selling something.'"

"I guess that makes sense," he said, as he wrote out a check. "But somehow it seems less professional."

If I'd known better, I would have told Wendell then and there that he was mistaken. Being obscure or turgid doesn't make anyone a professional—just ask my editor.

Unfortunately, though, the practice of law is *old* and we're stuck with a lot of antiquated and arcane language and procedure because of it. *Billa Exoneratonis. Hereditas damnosa.* They sound like curses you'd find in Hogwarts texts, right?

Leaping from a darkened alcove, Draco pointed his wand at Harry, shouting, "Hereditas damnosa!" Harry's body slumped to the ground, a soft pyramid of flesh, the curse having turned every bone in his body to rubber.

However, the larynx is not constructed of bone. It's constructed of cartilage, and with his last breath, Harry croaked, "Billa exoneratonis!" and was fully restored. Stupid Malfoy. He should never have sluffed his anatomy class that day.

Well, I wish it were so. These terms, in fact, simply deal with creditor and inheritance rights back in ancient Rome. They have no real use today, but there they are, hanging around in *Black's Law Dictionary*[1] like dusty webs in the ceiling of a warehouse. I wish we could sweep them, and a thousand terms like them, away. Sadly, I don't have that power, but hopefully I have the power to help you understand what the terms mean.

Abuse of Process: This means using court procedures to obtain a result that is unlawful or beyond the scope of a procedural rule. For example, having a summons served against someone just to try to intimidate them and not because you really want to have a trial. Put another way, abuse of process is like self-abuse. You have this handy tool that is designed for a specific purpose, and you use it for something entirely different just to have your way.

Advisement: Whenever you hear a judge say, "There are complex issues presented in this case that I need to reflect upon, so I am taking this case under advisement," what we're really saying is, "Whoa, I'm in over my head—this is my first medical malpractice case (or whatever), and I don't know what the hell to do, so I need more time." *Advisement* is a word that makes us sound way smarter than you.

I first used it in a small claims case in Beaver, Utah. One farmer was suing another for killing his cow. The cow had grazed in the wrong field one time too many, so the second farmer grabbed a tool—a shovel, if memory serves me—and swung it like a baseball bat, killing the cow with a single blow between the eyes. The farmers came directly from work to court—one in bib overalls grimed with soil, which impressed me—the two of them unknowingly parking their pickups next to mine as we all pulled in to the court lot just in time for the trial. They both looked capable of lifting a bale of hay with each hand. I, myself, was only up to a half-bale, or maybe a sheaf, so when the case was over and they glowered at me awaiting my verdict, I announced I was taking the case under advisement (even though I knew how I was going to rule), knowing I would likely never see them again. You might think of me as cowardly. I think of me as still alive.

Arraignment: This is when a judge tells you your rights and asks what your plea is to the charges. You should either say, "Guilty," or "Not guilty." The judge doesn't really care which. Really. Technically, there is also, "No Contest," but this is treated exactly the same on your record as a guilty plea and has absolutely no effect on your sentence. While it apparently makes people feel better about themselves because they didn't say the word "guilty," they are still agreeing to put a conviction on the record.

There is also a non-existent plea that I hear plucked out of the ether by misdemeanants at least once a month: "Guilty, Your Honor," they say, "but with an explanation!" The last part is delivered with a tone of anticipation, indicating that I will be knocked off the bench by its originality.

"Every guilty plea I've taken had an explanation," I tell them, duly noting their shocked expressions. The fact is, it's rare for anyone to take full blame for a crime, and everyone angles for a little lenience at sentencing.

My bet is that things weren't much different when the first crime on earth was committed:

God: "Adam, what is your plea to the charge of Falling to Temptation?"
Adam: "Guilty. But with an explanation!"
God: "And what would that be?"
Adam: "We were naked, and Eve is *hot!*"

Cautionary Instruction: This is a judge's instruction to jurors to disregard certain evidence. This comes up most often when something out of line is attempted by an attorney or witness, like trying to introduce evidence that is improper or has been excluded by the judge. Attorneys walk a fine line on this. If they get too aggressive, like mentioning an invalidly obtained confession, they risk mistrial or personal sanctions by the judge (and no one wants to retry a case). On the other hand, I know at least one law professor who told students it was a good tactic if you could get away with it, because if it's dynamite stuff, the judge telling the jurors to ignore it "would be like telling them to ignore the red-hot poker that just got shoved into their eye." A more genteel representation of the same thought is that, "You can't unring the bell." Yet try we do, us judges, so we don't have to start over from square one on a multiday trial.

Common Sense: This is not a legal term but is sometimes quoted as such by new lawyers and small claims litigants. The term is thrown at an opponent as if it was a knockout punch and the judge will raise the arm of the declarant as the winner of the bout. When a judge asks, "Do you have *any* evidence or law supporting your position?" and you reply, "It's just common sense, Your Honor," you might just as well start packing your briefcase. Unless, of course, the other side is saying the same thing. In which case the argument pretty much goes:

"It's just common sense, Your Honor."

"It is not."

"Is too."

"Is not."

In which case the judge has to rule on what *he* or *she* thinks is common sense.

And we all know *that's* a frightening prospect.

Constitutionalists: These are people who have access to the Internet and copy machines and who share their patriotic ideas with each other. They are characterized by a strong belief in the basic right to RANDOM CAPITALIZATION in their writings, the use of the term *admiralty law* in landlocked states, the right of all Americans to ignore traffic laws because of the Uniform Commercial Code, and an obsession with the thread color on flag borders—all of which are apparently covered by the Constitution of the United States of America. Who knew?

Evidence: Evidence is the facts of the case as introduced through exhibits and testimony. Sometimes after a jury trial, a new attorney will ask me, "What did I do wrong?" I don't bother mentioning the things that afflict all first-timers—like wearing a new suit with the labels still sewn to the back of the sleeves, being so nervous that they get the names of the parties mixed up, and twisting themselves into verbal pretzels. Instead, I'll give them my opinion on something that could be a recurring problem if I thought I saw one, but just as often I say they did *nothing* wrong—they just didn't have the facts on their side. I don't think style wins out over substance. None of us are as smooth and resplendent as actors in a courtroom movie. (This isn't to say an attorney or *pro se* litigant can just sit back and expect their evidence to present itself and win the case. Preparation is key.) We're not talking about just my opinion here. I meet with jurors after a verdict. More than once they have said the attorney for the prevailing party didn't do a good job, or that the losing attorney did a really good job—they just thought the plaintiff or defendant should prevail based on the evidence. What a concept.

This point was actually brought home to me just before closing arguments in a jury trial when I was a prosecutor. The defense counsel was a law school friend of mine.

As the judge instructed the jury, my opponent leaned over to me and whispered, "If you had any balls, you'd do what a prosecutor did to me in a jury trial in Salt Lake last week. His entire closing argument was: 'My case is so strong I'm not going to say anything. I'm just curious to hear what *he* has to say,' pointing at me. And then he just sat down."

"We've been friends for a long time, Ron," I said. "You know I don't have any balls." Then, while he groaned, I gave my closing argument and the jury convicted the defendant, and I closed my prosecutorial career 1–0 against my friend. It was not because I was the more skillful trial lawyer. It helps if the guy you're prosecuting for drunk driving thinks he's at an intersection when there isn't one for another one hundred yards, executes a perfect left turn, embedding himself into a ditch, and then blows an air sample so high that the breathalyzer needs a full twenty-four hours to dry out.

Illegitimate Children: Okay, not the word we're *really* after here, but I'll get to that in a minute. On my first day as a law clerk for the Utah Attorney General, the supervising attorney gave me what he thought was an easy task: researching a question about requiring men who fathered children out of wedlock to pay child support. I looked in the Utah Code index under *out-of-wedlock children*. Nothing. I tried *illegitimate children, unmarried fathers, unmarried mothers* . . . basically any combination of terms that came to mind. No dice. Then I went to *American Jurisprudence* and *Corpus Juris Secundum*. I was getting nowhere. I'd wasted an hour when I crawled back to the attorney expecting to be sacked for being so damn dumb.

"That was quick," he said, impressed. "Let's see what you have."

"Nothing," I said, and explained my search.

He went back to his paperwork, motioned to the door, and said, "Look under *bastards*."

"You've gotta be kidding me," I thought. *Bastards?* Then, as I walked toward the library, I began wondering if I was being hazed as a new clerk, like sending a tenderfoot on a snipe hunt. But nope—when I looked in the same indexes, right there under *bastards* was all kinds of gold to be mined.

I wondered then, and I still do: is this the best we can do for children who, through no fault of their own, have unmarried parents? We call them bastards? Let's be honest here—the definition we all think of, and that is contained in your regular dictionary is, "a vicious, despicable, or thoroughly disliked person." *Webster's Dictionary* keeps up with vernacular changes, so why can't *Black's Law Dictionary* and legal encyclopedias? You'd think the legal text editors would make the change, and under *bastards* you'd read, *see out-of-wedlock*. But they don't. There's only one word to describe people like that, and you know what it is.

Legal Tender: "The money (bills and coins) approved in a country for the payment of debts."[2] Pretty simple concept, right? Well, not always.

Once, as a prosecutor, I was visiting a judge in his chambers when we were interrupted by a loud crash and yelling just outside his door. He charged out to find a huge pile of pennies on the counter and an irate man yelling at his clerk. The judge and I immediately recognized the man: he'd been convicted of a misdemeanor the previous week. He turned to the judge and announced that he was paying his $300 fine with thirty thousand pennies. With a grin on his face, he headed back to his car for more. The judge went ballistic, saying he wasn't going to have his clerk spend the rest of the day putting pennies in coin rolls. The defendant stood his ground for a while, spewing a mantra about the *Magna Carta* and the right to pay his debt using "the coin of the realm" or some such thing. The judge said he'd jail the man if he didn't pick up all the coins, *right now.* The man eventually caved, not because he'd come to his senses, but because an armed bailiff joined us. (I don't know if the judge's threat was a technical abuse of judicial discretion, but as a taxpayer, I liked the conclusion.)

Years later, as a judge, I had a case where a physically intimidating man exposed himself to a ten-year-old girl on a Sunday morning as she walked to church. The child was traumatized, and therapy was necessary. As a part of his sentence, I ordered the defendant to reimburse the child's parents for any out-of-pocket counseling fees. At a probation review I saw that this hadn't happened. I asked the defendant why I shouldn't put him in jail for the failure.

"I tried to pay, but he won't take my money," he said, motioning to the victim's father.

"Surely that's not right, is it?" I asked the father.

"He tried to pay me with a check," the father said. "I'm entitled to be paid in gold." Then he went on about how the federal government should have never gone off the gold standard. I let him vent for a few minutes, but when he wanted to explain how FDR had led the nation astray, I cut him off, saying, "Mr. Johnson, (not his real name) I know you and your family. I know you are a smart man. (He was a licensed engineer, and I'd been childhood friends with his older brother.) But what you are saying is just plain dumb. I'll make the defendant pay in cash or by check, but I won't make him pay you in gold bullion." He glowered at me and never accepted a dime. It's not often that the man who exposed himself would come across as the less crazy one.

Why do people take a bad situation and make it worse? My take is that some, like Mr. Johnson, honestly hold to principles they believe are correct, and when they conflict with reality, they lose out. More often, like Pennypacker, they are just hard-wired jerks who think they can always bully their way through life. Either way, a judge is there to say, enough is enough, and draw a reasonable line in the sand. Even with legal tender.

Ludicrous: Actually, this is a word used by some big city people. (In southern Utah, we prefer the all-purpose phrase *fer ignernt* to denigrate something an opponent has said). For example, "It is *ludicrous* for opposing counsel to even suggest that my client was having an affair." By doing this, though, the speaker unwittingly alerts the trial judge and jury that we will be dealing with at least one emotionally overwrought person, that being the lawyer who just made this "ignernt" declaration.

Perjury: This is lying under oath. It's a felony, but it's also the court system's dirty little secret. I was shocked when I became a judge and realized that it happens on an almost daily basis and is almost never prosecuted.

I don't mean testimony involving honest people having differing opinions based on their perspective and ability to see and remember events. That, too, happens all the time. I'm talking about the situation where the landlord says he was never paid April's rent, and the tenant says he paid cash and handed it to the landlord in person, and it happened just two months ago, so someone is lying. Or the drunk driver who says he'd only had "two beers," despite the fact he couldn't touch his nose or recite the alphabet—you get the picture. Why isn't perjury prosecuted more often? Because of that "proof beyond a reasonable doubt" thing (stay tuned—definition coming). And it bugs the heck out of me, but who's going to file a case you can't win?

Not that I've been above lying now and then in my life when I felt so compelled. I just don't do it under oath. The first memorable lie was seared into my memory when I was a third-grader and my school had a program for kids to subscribe to *The Weekly Reader* over the summer recess. I took the form home, filled it out, and showed it to my mother. "Could I please have money for this program?" No problem—what a wonderful boy I was to want to read like that over the summer.

I pocketed the couple of bucks she gave me, got on my bike, and rode to a tiny neighborhood store a stone's throw from the school. I walked in, and—for the first time in my whole life—bought an entire unopened carton of *Topp's* baseball cards—one hundred and twenty cards, twenty-four packs with five cards each. They came in five-cent packs with a thin, tasteless slab of bubble gum. The whole thing cost $1.20. As I rode home, I felt as if I'd won about the greatest prize a person could have. I opened them when it was safe in my room in the basement, and I blended them into my existing collection by teams.

The glow didn't last long. First, Mom wondered why the *Weekly Reader* wasn't arriving. "Don't worry," I said. "It's just a mistake." Then she felt sorry for me because I was so looking forward to reading them. "It's okay," I said. "I can read my other books." Then she was about to talk to the teacher—a friend of hers—about the problem. She was ready to bust wide-open this *Weekly Reader* scam of ripping off innocent little readers. I had to come clean.

She just stared at me, hurt and bewildered. Her trustworthy little packrat had embezzled from her. The punishment was chores to pay back twice the amount of money she had given me. I thought it was pretty fair.

***Pro Hac Vice*:** Latin again, meaning "for this occasion." When an out-of-state attorney wants to represent a client in another state, he must file a *Pro Hac Vice* Motion. Then the judge decides if he should be allowed to enter that case. *Pro Hac Vice* is to be pronounced, "Pro-hawk-vee-chay," which is pretty peculiar if you ask me. *Vice* is pronounced "vee-chay?" Seriously? Lust is one of the seven deadly *vee-chays*? The Vee-chay Squad is going to bust the pimps and prostitutes? That makes no sense, so I don't give in to this elitist pronunciation. I just pronounce it the way it is spelled: "Pro-hack-vice" and then watch the visiting attorneys' eyes light up as they think, *All right! I got me a real bumpkin here! I can run circles around this guy.*

My family says sometimes I latch onto things that bother me and harp about them much too long. They say it is one of *my* vices. But they're wrong of course, because technically, I have no vices. Just vee-chays.

***Pro se* litigant:** This is someone who represents himself in court. This occurs because the person can't afford an attorney or because they think they can do a better job than an attorney (*rarely* the case) or because it's just small claims or a traffic case. By all means, have at it as a wan-nabe attorney on the last two. Just please, please don't behave like you're auditioning for a part on *Law and Order*. A new briefcase or pinstripe suit isn't going to inject jurisprudence into your brain. Stick to what you know, and present your facts politely and confidently. But if you're in an area where you're in over your head, don't try to fake it with bombast and swagger—that's like heralding your performance with trumpets to make sure everyone noticed you're wearing the emperor's new clothes.

Finally, *pro se* litigants usually don't know rules of procedure, or rules of evidence, and this frustrates everyone in the courtroom (except maybe the other side, who was smart enough to hire a lawyer). *Pro se* litigants often count on the judge to help them out.

"What would you do if you were my lawyer?" their eyes seem to ask. "What questions should I ask this witness?"

But a judge can no more do that than a referee can look at the score-board, think "Oh, poor Slippery Rock University is getting their ass kicked," and then trip the Alabama tailback on his way to the end zone to even things up. Don't count on a David v. Goliath result if you've never used a slingshot.

Questions: This the most common mistake laymen make when coming to traffic court or small claims court. For example:

Judge: "You will get a chance to tell your story after the prosecution has rested. But for now, do you have any *questions* you want to ask this witness?"

Defendant: "Yes!" they say, moving in for the kill. "I couldn't have been going forty-five, officer, because I was in second gear!"

Judge: "That's not a question; it's a statement. Save it for your testimony on the witness stand."

Defendant: "Okay. Sorry. I'm not a lawyer or anything. So, officer, I know I wasn't speeding because I looked at my speedometer, and it only read thirty-five miles per hour!"

And so it goes. Just for the record, here is the definition: "*Question*: a sentence in an interrogative form, addressed to someone in order to get information in reply."[3]

Reasonable Doubt: The highest standard of proof in our court system. It's the burden of proof the prosecution must pass to get a conviction. It's a tough standard to define, and there are a bunch of equally confusing definitions out there. Here's one used in a lot of courts, including my state court, since the Utah Supreme Court approved it in the 1990s:

"A reasonable doubt is a doubt based on reason and one which is reasonable in view of all the evidence. It must be reasonable doubt and not a doubt which is merely fanciful or imaginary or based on wholly speculative possibility. Proof beyond a reasonable doubt is that degree of proof which satisfies the mind, convinces the understanding of those who are bound to act conscientiously upon it, and prevents all reasonable doubt."

This language always struck me as being disturbingly similar to the *Mr. Ed* theme song ("A horse is a horse, of course of course, unless the horse . . ." or however that song went.) If you looked at the jurors at this point, you would know who has been listening—those with the *Say what?* expressions on their faces. I'm happy to report that after my retirement the instruction was modified by the Utah Supreme Court in State v. Reyes, (2005), and a more understandable definition was included in Utah's MUJI—Model Utah Jury Instructions.

One final note on this for laymen and especially for headline writers: no jury ever found a defendant "innocent." (The defendant may, in fact, *be* innocent, but that's not what the jury was asked to determine.) They found him or her "not guilty." This is *not* splitting hairs. More than once, I have told a defendant after a bench trial: "I can understand why the policeman arrested you, and I think there's a better than fifty percent chance you committed this crime, but I'm finding you 'not guilty' because I can't say that the case against you has been proven beyond a reasonable doubt." Some European courts use the phrase "not proven." Perhaps that is a more exact phrase.

Subpoena: I think this word is so familiar it's entered the modern lexicon. A subpoena is a document that forces you to testify. But when used in the plural form, with other Latin words, you get mutations like the following:

- *Subpoenas Duces Tecum*: This means you have to bring things like documents to court for examination. So, you'd think we could just go ahead and call them a *Document Subpoena*, or *Subpoena for the Production of Documents*. But we can't. If we did, a businessman wouldn't have to call up his attorney and say, "What in the hell is a *subpoena duces tecum*?" And then, billable hours would not be generated. (See *Res Judicata*.) And we can't have that.

- *Subpoena ad testificandum*: This is a subpoena ordering a witness to appear and testify. "Wait a minute," you're thinking. "Isn't that the same as subpoena?" The answer is yes.

Voir Dire: If you are in the jury pool, you will probably hear the judge ask the attorneys if they have any questions on *voir dire*. *Voir dire* questions are those asked of jurors so that attorneys can intelligently remove potential jurors with improper perspectives and biases that would hurt their clients (*bad* jurors), and select jurors with proper perspectives and biases that will be favorable to their clients (*good* jurors). This ensures an *impartial* jury—or so the thinking goes. I'm told *voir dire* is properly pronounced: "Vwaaah-dear." But if the judge says it that way, he sounds like a fancy-pants, and the regular Joes on the jury will snicker. On the other hand, if the judge says it the other way (like me), "Vore-die-yerr," all multi-syllabic and slowly drawn out, he sounds like a hick, and attorneys will suspect he tracked manure on the carpet when he entered the courtroom. So I guess either way he's in trouble.

BLACK'S TERMS TO BREAK OUT AT COCKTAIL PARTIES:

Bilboes: Shackles used at sea. (*Not* hobbits!)

Burking: *n.* The crime of murdering someone, usually by smothering, for the purpose of selling the corpse. *This term arose from the Scottish murder team of Burke and Hare, whose practice in 1828 of suffocating their victims while leaving few visible marks made the corpses more salable to medical schools. –**burke,** *vb.*

Defossion: The punishment of being buried alive.

Gamalis: A child born to betrothed but unmarried parents—Need we be this nitpicky?

Lollipop syndrome: "A situation in which one parent in a custody battle provides the child with fun, gifts, and good times and leaves all matters of discipline to the other parent." In other words, where a parent acts like your average grandparent.

Pettifogger: A lawyer lacking common sense. (As if *that* could happen!)

Slayers rule: You can't inherit from someone you slayed. Tell your kids they'll just have to wait.

Trigamy: Three wives. But it ends there—there isn't a quadramy for four wives and pentamy for five wives and so on, so I have absolutely no idea what Brigham Young was with his fifty-five wives.

TERMS USEFUL IN OFFICE AND BOARD MEETINGS:

Ad Rectum: To meet an accusation.

Aunt Jemima Doctrine: The principle that a trademark is protected not only from an act of direct copying, but also from the use of any similar mark that would likely make a buyer think that the item bearing the similar mark comes from the same source as the trademarked item.

Bathtub Conspiracy: A conspiracy by subsidiaries of the same company.

Damn-Fool Doctrine: Where courts refuse insurance coverage for acts too ill conceived to allow the actor to transfer the risk of such conduct to an insurer. This is a close relative of the Step-in-the-Dark rule. (You can't wander around in an unfamiliar, pitch-black area and then sue the owner if you hurt yourself.)

Pac-Man Defense: Company A attempts to takeover Company B and ends up being gobbled up instead.

Sanction: Means two totally contradictory things: (1) authorize, (2) punish. Kind of like on the Simpsons when a firecracker blows up a gas tank and Dr. Nick says, "Inflammable means flammable? What a country!"[4]

Scintilla of Evidence: This is defined as the slightest amount or a trace. For example, "There is not a *scintilla of evidence* that I was once a pettifogger!"

Sergeant Shultz Defense: "An assertion by a criminal who claims . . . that he knew nothing, saw nothing, and heard nothing."[5] Yup. From *Hogan's Heroes*, and it's in *Black's Law Dictionary*.

TERMS THAT SMELL OF INNUENDO:

Arrears: When you haven't paid rent like you should your payments are "in arrears." Once, I dictated a standard dunning letter to a new secretary to send to a tenant. Good I proofread the letter before signing it, because she had me threatening the renter with a lawsuit because their rent payments "were in the rears."

CUPOS: Cohabiting Unmarried Person of the Opposite Sex.

Faggot: Firewood.

On All Fours: No, it's not "how dogs run," it's "squarely on point."

Sleeping Partner: Secret partner.

SODDI Defense: "Some Other Dude Did It." Honest. It's in there.

In fact, let's get those terms that smell of innuendo—but aren't—out of the way right now: In Delicto, Date of Cleavage, Jury Box, Lay Day, Love Day, *de anno bisextili*, Penal Redress, Hung jury, Heirs of the Body, and Hors. These do not mean what your dirty mind might think.

"The Law is a Jealous Mistress." I first heard this phrase on the opening day of law school. The dean gave a bracing speech to all of us frightened freshmen telling us of the long hours of study that lay ahead, the challenging questions that would be fired at us by the erudite professors who would brook no namby-pamby answers—basically the John Houseman speech from *The Paper Chase* movie that came out six months later. I was scared at first, then bored from all the chest-thumping, and then dismissive when he concluded by saying, "Your personal life will suffer because the law is a jealous mistress!"

Only if your personal life is already screwed up, I thought to myself. If you're willing to abandon your spouse because you prefer textbooks and professors, there's something wrong at home. Four months later, I got married. Arlene and I both studied hard and mixed in recreation and time together—and I never came within a country mile of making law review. When you're not a genius, you have to allocate your time the best you can.

So the next time you hear an unfamiliar, ominous phrase, don't flinch and look over your shoulder. Voldemort isn't about to attack—it's just us lawyers exercising our arcane craft.

NOTES

1. *Black's Law Dictionary*, 7th ed. (St. Paul: West Group, 1999).
2. Ibid.
3. *The Random House Dictionary of the English Language*, unabridged ed. (New York: Random House, 1966), s.v. "question."
4. Matt Selman, "Trilogy of Error," *The Simpsons*, episode 18, season 12, directed by Mike B. Anderson, aired April 29, 2001.
5. *Black's Law Dictionary*. 7th ed. (St. Paul: West Group, 1999).

Appendix

I am a federal magistrate. When a shackled defendant shows up in my court for the first time and is charged with a felony, I have to decide if he should stay in jail until trial or be released with certain conditions. I don't just pull this decision out of thin air. I make it after reviewing an official Pretrial Services Report from the court's probation officer, who is proficient in such matters. The reports are formatted with boxes and columns chock full of relevant details: family history, prior arrests, education background, and other useful things like that.

I am also a writer. Approaching New York agents and publishers with my first manuscript (an earlier book), I found that in the publishing world, the burden of proof is reversed from what I'm used to: I'm presumed guilty—of being a fraud—until proven innocent. Labels shrieking, "UNAGENTED MATERIAL—RETURN TO SENDER!" were slapped on my unopened query letter envelopes—as if anthrax spores have been stuffed inside—and returned to me, presumably in disgust.

What those guarding the publishing gates need is what I get as a sitting judge: information. More specifically: information presented in a safe, standardized format. Forget query letters. What editors and their slush pile minions should see is a version of a Pretrial Services Report— a Pre-Submission Services Report, if you will—containing the same basic background about me that I receive about criminal defendants. An effective summation using public records and information from a family member would be very helpful. If I'm going to be viewed as a criminal, my thinking goes, at least have the decency to treat me like one.

PRE-SUBMISSION SERVICES REPORT

District/Office
New York/ NYC

Charge(s)
1. Fraudulent use of a PC.
2. Impersonating a writer.
3. Expressing an opinion from the hinterlands.

Arresting Officer's Probable Cause Statement: Defendant is writing a book about his experiences as a judge. The book purports to offer up some observations about life, human nature, and human fallibility. Defendant is unpublished and uncredentialed, yet expects to be taken seriously, so unintended humor abounds.

DEFENDANT HISTORY

1. DEFENDANT'S HISTORY/FAMILY/EMPLOYMENT:

Defendant was born in Ithaca, New York, but he pretty much spent the rest of his life exiled to Cedar City, Utah. He washed dishes at the Grand Canyon at age sixteen, ran the elevator in the Washington Monument as a college student, and floundered through law school cursing the Socratic Method rather than going with the flow. Married, his wife/enabler (an artist) rationalizes defendant's current windmill tilting, by saying, "Oh, let him write. It doesn't hurt anyone, and it strokes his ego!" Four children. Youngest child, Hope, is a codefendant in an earlier case (see prior offenses, below).

Defendant was a city attorney and then a state trial judge, and then he retired to become a part-time US magistrate judge. In other words, a cipher slobbering his way around the government trough.

Defendant presently hears criminal cases arising in the southern half of Utah—with many cases coming from national parks, Forest Service, BLM land, and Lake Powell. It's a vast area with a wide smattering of crimes and people. He also hears cases in Salt Lake City regularly.

2. FINANCIAL RESOURCES:

The defendant makes a decent wage from his employment. He doesn't *have* to do what he is trying to do. But then, what criminal does?

3. PHYSICAL AND MENTAL HEALTH:

On the one hand, defendant reported he is in good physical health, and is not taking any medication or using health equipment for any serious problems. Then, in the next breath, he admits ingesting physician-prescribed blood pressure pills, pills to ward off irregular heartbeats, and a diuretic pill so his ears don't ring; describes having to affix a large, rubber CPAP mask to his face at night to ward off sleep apnea; and admits occasionally downing near-lethal doses of ibuprofen for arthritis after those days when he hikes, which he does, he says, because he is, "young at heart" (presumably the one he takes pills for). Despite this, he says he has never undergone psychiatric treatment, been in mental health counseling, nor contemplated suicide. Which, of course, begs the question, "Why not?"

4. PRIOR RECORD:

The following information is based solely on self-reporting by defendant. Understandably, publishers and agents haven't advertised dealing with him in the past.

Crime: Impersonating a Writer (2007). Status: Convicted.

Defendant self-published a book, *With Hope across America: A Father-Daughter Journey*, after being considered, but rejected by a number of prominent publishers. One New York editor candidly emailed him, "Hope seems to be such a grounded and generally good kid (congrats and thanks to you!), which, ironically, makes the story a little less interesting than it might be if she had troubles you'd set out to help solve on this trip. As sorry as I am to say this, the truth is you've done a great job raising your daughter, and there's no conflict here."

Reading this, one wonders, "No incest, no addiction problems, no violence—what was the idiot thinking?" Yet, when confronted with this email together with other rejection letters, defendant refuses to learn anything.

"I don't think the level of writing killed the book," he whines. "I think it was the fact that no one gives a crap what someone from Utah thinks about the rest of the country."

In mitigation, it should be noted that positive blurbs were somehow obtained from the eclectic group of honest citizens and authors: Bill McKibben, Jason F. Wright, Michael C. Keith, and Jamie Jensen.

Crime: Impersonating a Writer (2010). Status: Convicted.
Upon the advice of the agent for his first book (what was he smoking?), the defendant set out on more journeys with his daughter, which resulted in yet another two-person, two-generation, two-gender look at a country, in this case, *Smitten By Canada: Another %!@^! Travel Memoir.* This time he mercifully dumped it on the slag-heap of self-published corpses spending minimal money on photocopying and postage.

Crime: Impersonating a Writer. (2014). Status: Present Offense.
Defendant is alleged to be at it again, but with a new angle, writing about his experiences as a judge. When contacted at university and told her father was attempting yet another book, Hope gushed, "Thank you, God. At least it's not, *With Hope in the Dormitory: A Daughter's Emotional Suffocation!*"

When asked why he continues to write despite his failures, the defendant quickly deflected, claiming that his first book inspired his eldest child to become an author.

Note: While Allyson Braithwaite Condie (Ally Condie), author of the best-selling *Matched* trilogy, gives a different version of events, telling this investigator, "When I saw Dad writing a book, I thought, 'Hell, if *he* can write a book, anyone can, and I got off my butt.'"

5. NEED-TO-REJECT ASSESSMENT:
Risk of Manuscript Submission: High. But the defendant is considered to be a manageable risk based on the following:
- Nature and circumstances of the instant offence: While delusional and relentless, the defendant is relatively harmless.

Risk of loss of existing customers: Low. The defendant is considered to be a manageable risk of danger based on the following:

- Nature and circumstances of the instant offense: he's likely to just toss it on the self-published slag heap (see 6b above).
- Criminal History: Since no one reads his drivel, it's hard to find any actual victims.

RECOMMENDATION

It is the position of Pre-Publication Services, that there are conditions that will reasonably assure the safety of the publishing community. Therefore, it is respectfully recommended the defendant not be rejected on sight so long as he agrees to comply with the following special conditions:

1. Make one submission only of the current manuscript, contingent on defendant's understanding that,
2. Under Publishing's strict, "Three-Strikes Rule," if he fails this time, he's out for good.

Publisher's Note: Even with the author's acknowledged faults, we felt a third strike should not be called, and that this book should see the light of day.

ABOUT THE AUTHOR
Robert Braithwaite

In a twenty-seven year judicial career, Robert Braithwaite has been a circuit judge, a district judge, a juvenile judge, a pro tem Utah Supreme Court judge, and is now a US magistrate judge. He has heard cases ranging from parking tickets to rape and murder. As a part-time magistrate judge, he now hears criminal cases arising in the southern half of Utah, usually occurring in national parks, national forests, and federal lands. Needless to say, he rides a circuit, hearing cases in four diverse locations: St. George, Big Water, Moab, and Salt Lake City.

He lives in Cedar City with his wife, who is an artist. Together they have raised four children.